HOW TO CATCH THE
BIGGEST TROUT
OF YOUR LIFE

HOW TO CATCH THE
BIGGEST TROUT
OF YOUR LIFE

Landon Mayer

Photography by the author and others
Fly photography by Ted Fauceglia

Illustrations by Greg Pearson

WILD
RIVER
PRESS

Library of Congress Cataloging-in-Publication Data
Mayer, Landon.
    How to catch the biggest trout of your life/Landon Mayer.—1st ed.
      p. cm.
    ISBN 9780974642765 (hardcover)
Fly fishing. 2. Trout. I. Title.

    2004117106

Book and jacket design by Gregory Smith Design
Photographs of flies and materials by Ted Fauceglia
Fishing photos by the author and others

Published by Wild River Press, Post Office Box 13360, Mill Creek,
Washington 98082 USA

Wild River Press Web site address: www.wildriverpress.com

Printed in China through Colorcraft Ltd., Hong Kong

10 9 8 7 6 5 4 3 2 1

DEDICATION

This book is dedicated to the memory of my Grandma, Jessie Lillian Mayer, whose love and support throughout my life made me the person I am today. I enjoyed reliving my fly-fishing adventures by sharing them with her, and watching the sparkle my stories brought to her eyes. She taught me that life is what you make of it, but in the end love is what matters.

Landon Mayer

ACKNOWLEDGEMENTS

I am grateful to my family: my mom, Robbie; brother Sean; sister Lauren; sister-in-law Kira; nephew Julian; nieces Amelie and Cossete; and to Nikki, Bianca, Angelina and Alex. Thank you for your patience, love, support of my career, and of this work. You are always there for me, and your encouragement during the creation of this book was no exception.

My daughter, Madelyn—you are my favorite gal whom I love with all of my heart. I have new meaning in life because of you, and you inspire me to be at my best every day, on and off of the water.

Jennifer O'Neal, whose affection, love, encouragement, and sacrifice of many late nights at the computer with me made this book come to life.

My friend Scottie Miller—without your friendship, fortitude and knowledge in writing and editing, this book would not be possible. You make me strive to be first-rate in every walk of life. Thank you!

My friend John Barr—who shares my drive and enthusiasm for the sport of fly fishing. Your belief in me has opened new doors, and I am grateful for our friendship.

Eric Mondragon, Matt Wilkerson, Jay Harper, Angus Drummond, Dennis Kreutz, John Burger, Jack Talon and Frank Martin—our friendship and our time in waders is dear to me. Each fishing adventure we have is filled with the knowledge and excitement reflected in this book. I am thankful to have met and to know each of you.

Brad, Sherri and Bill Tomlinson, and Dick Rock, whose closeness, help, and affection over the years have opened the door to this life of fly fishing that I love. Making me a part of your family inside and outside The Peak Fly Shop means so much.

Tony Gibson with Colorado Fishing Adventures—your friendship and bracing strength are always present. Your kindness in the stream and on land is contagious.

CONTENTS

FOREWORD

FOUR HOURS AGO I HOISTED A BEAUTIFUL 16-POUND BROWN trout out of the river. An hour earlier I landed a 14-pounder in the same run. I have Landon Mayer to thank for both of them. He not only spotted the fish for me, but kept an eye on them from the far bank while I cast to them. It was "buddy-system" fishing at its best.

More than any angler I have ever met, Landon has an uncanny knack for finding and catching trophy trout. He consistently lands more big fish each year than most experienced anglers find in a lifetime of fishing. I don't know how he does it—only that he does. And he loves teaching others how to do the same. His enthusiasm is as exciting as it is contagious.

I first met Landon in 2004 at the Fly Fishing Show in Denver, Colorado. I was standing next to the Sage booth, visiting with my good friends, Jerry Siem and Marc Bale, and I spotted him across the aisle. I recognized Landon from a picture of him I had seen in the *Denver Post* a few months earlier.

The photo appeared in Charlie Myers's outdoor column, and showed Landon holding a record 30-inch, 11-pound brown caught on the South Platte River. The fish was an International Game Fish Association state record for the largest brown trout caught on a four- pound test leader. The caption mentioned that the fish was caught on October 12, 2004 on a size 20 Copper John—my pattern. It was something of a thrill for me to hear. I remember thinking that it would be fun to meet Landon someday, and here he was standing 20 feet away, so I knew I needed to take advantage of the opportunity.

I introduced myself and congratulated him on his record catch. Then we made small talk for the next 30 minutes or so. Landon and I hit it off immediately. We learned that we had fished a lot of the same waters and shared a lot of similar interests and experiences. He was a genuinely nice guy, which was refreshing. Before parting ways, we decided to hook up some day and fish together in one of our favorite Colorado waters. A couple of weeks later I decided to follow through, so I gave him a call. We set a date to fish a prime spot on the Yampa River.

When angers say they're going to fish together, normally they meet at the water, trade a few niceties, then take off on their own to find a patch of water. They might come back together when one of them gets a tight line, but right after the photo they head back to their own hole. With Landon and me it was nothing like that. We spent the day actually fishing together. We took turns sighting out a nice trout then one of us would keep an eye on him while the other threw to him. When one of us had a fish on we'd celebrate together. I've always enjoyed the camaraderie of fishing almost as much as the catching, and it was clear that Landon felt the same way. It was one more thing we had in common.

Around noon a thunderstorm rolled in, so we made our way to the car and traded fish stories until the clouds parted. We wolfed down a few power bars and laughed ourselves silly. Then when the rains passed, we made our way back to the river where I hooked a beautiful eight-pound rainbow while Landon netted him and took a killer photo for me. It was a great bit of topping on a truly memorable day of fishing. I knew then and there that Landon was my kind of angler.

That was the first of many days of fishing we've shared over the last few years. But more than that, it was the beginning of a great friendship—one that I'm sure will last many years.

I'm thrilled at the opportunity to endorse both Landon and his first book, not just because he is a treasured friend, but a truly stellar fly fisher. His ability to sight and land trophy trout is nothing short of spectacular—not to mention fun to watch. In fact, I've nicknamed Landon "the Osprey," because no one spots fish better.

I also can't imagine a more appropriate title. *How to Catch the Biggest Trout of Your Life* is exactly what you can expect to learn from what you are about to read. And I can't think of anyone more qualified to teach it than Landon. I'm just glad he's finished writing—maybe now we can get back to the water and fish!

JOHN BARR
BOULDER, COLORADO
October 2006

INTRODUCTION

AFTER A DAY OF FLY FISHING FOR TROUT, most of us talk about two things: how many we caught, and the largest fish of the day. Then there's the one that got away. Fish long enough and we all experience—or hope to experience—that unforgettable encounter with an elusive trophy trout. I've caught my share and more. But not a single one came easily. During thousands of hours on the water, through trial and error and failure and success, I've concluded that landing a giant trout doesn't have to be the rare "chance of a lifetime." Instead, your fishing can become a lifetime of chances.

Persistence is vital. So is dedication. And so is knowledge. That's why I decided to write this book. I am convinced that by following the basic steps I've discovered for pursuing trophy trout, you too can be successful. The quest starts by recognizing that there's a difference between "going fishing" and going after possibly the biggest trout of your life.

In what you are about to read, I've held nothing back. My aim is to share with you in clear, concise language—with the tremendous aid of angler-artist Greg Pearson's excellent illustrations—everything I've learned.

These are the techniques and strategies I've developed, the ones I use when I'm on my favorite rivers. Collectively, as a guide, this information offers the serious angler a practical, repeatable process for pursuing and landing trophy trout.

The key to unlocking much of the information in this book was achieved by paying my dues, and, most important, being open to learning something new every day on the water. I wasn't alone very often. Fly-fishing friends, co-workers, and passionate angling acquaintances I shared these adventures with helped make this book possible. I give many thanks for sharing many wonderful hours with these great individuals: Jennifer O'neal, Eric Mondragon, Matt Wilkerson, Jay Harper, Brad Tomlinson, Sherry Tomlinson, Scottie Miller, Dennis Kreutz, Dusty Sprague, Tony Gibson, Frank Martin, John Barr, George Spangler, Dick Rock, Hobbie Ragland, Steve Gossage, Gary Tibbets, Matt Bynum, Ed Engle and Phil Camera.

My sincere hope is that you will learn something valuable from this book. My greatest reward would be in knowing that I truly added to a fellow angler's fishing enjoyment. May what you're about to read lead you on a personal journey of success and excitement that the challenge of trophy trout offers.

Understanding
Trophy Trout

NOWING AS MUCH AS POSSIBLE about the species of fish you are targeting increases your chances of being where the fish are. It also allows you to understand their diet, feeding habits, and other behavior—information key to catching them.

I like to think of large trout almost as a different species when compared to the normal behavior of average-sized trout. Large trout have different body characteristics. They act differently and display different behavioral patterns. I frequently remind myself that these giants haven't become this big by pure luck. Understanding what adjustments they have made in their diets, where they live to survive, and how they behave— daily and seasonally—is important to your fishing success.

There are many distinctively visible characteristics between male and female trout. These differences in body structure are sometimes exaggerated, sometimes subtle. However, they all play a role in big-trout behavior and activity. The most common difference between male and female trout is the shape of their head and jaw.

BODY STRUCTURE

Large trout grow primarily in length during their early years of life. Then in their later years they gain weight by expanding girth—it's how true giants attain their exceptional proportions.

Both male and female trout have the potential to grow to substantial size. As they become huge, however, their shapes can vary markedly. Some trophies are long and lean, while some are shorter and fatter. Other big trout are thicker, while others are simply longer. Each waterway produces different growth in the fish residing there. When I fish where trophy trout have room to move or migrate, I have learned that these fish typically possess longer and leaner bodies. When trophies are in water where they are confined to 200-yard stretch their whole life, they tend to be shorter in length and larger in girth, becoming almost obese.

One day my fishing buddy Matt Wilkerson and I were in pursuit of trophy trout on the famous Taylor River in Colorado. About mid-afternoon, Matt hooked into a thick brown. The fish was deceptive. He hollered down to me, "Landon, I've got a big one." We often help one another out netting fish, as this can be an enormous advantage when you're dealing with strong, giant trout. When he was fighting the fish and it flashed sideways, we could plainly see its impressive girth. "*Big fish!*" we both thought. The fish moved into an upright position and now it looked to be just average. Matt continued playing the guessing game until he was ready to net it.

"It's big, well, maybe not, wait…it's big," he rattled. Then lo and behold, when we netted this brown, it was a fat fish—its length almost matching its girth. It was a saucer plate. The fish measured 17 inches long and 16 inches around. It had consumed so much protein it gave new meaning to the word obese. We couldn't believe it.

THE HEAD AND JAW

Male Trout

Male trout have the unique formation of an arrow-shaped head and jaw. This jaw formation is often referred to as its "kype." The kype is lined with a row of teeth and is a hard-based structure. The lower part of the jaw is extended slightly farther than the top. It has a nub at the tip, which allows the jaw to close and connect with the upper portion of the jaw. These formations of the male trout's jaw are typically oversized. Male trout develop a kype throughout the course of their life, but during the pre-spawn stage, the hormonal change of the male causes the kype to extend while exhibiting greater aggression.

I am reminded of a male brown trout I caught in upstate New York. I was able to see this fish in deep water because of the white glint of its jaw—something I look for when a trout is actively feeding and opens its mouth to inhale. When I landed this trophy, to my surprise the fish had one of the most ridiculous nubs I have ever seen on a male trout's jaw. I couldn't resist measuring it: two and a half inches long. It had grown so large it was curling back into its mouth. The fish literally could not close its mouth completely. That's why the white glint of its mouth was so apparent in deeper water. I had to laugh. *This fish won't have a problem opening its mouth to eat!* I thought.

When open, the males' jaws are considerably larger than the females'. This helps the male get more leverage when it bites down and also gives it more jaw area to bite with. There are two main purposes to these

This beautiful male brown trout—one of the cleanest I have seen—was the best birthday gift Sean Mayer ever received. My brother chased the fish 100 yards downstream. What gorgeous colors.

aggressive features on male trout. The first is to fend off other males from a spawning territory; male trout instinctively dart after each other when battling for spawning rights, biting each other to show dominance. Often it seems that the longer the male, the larger its head and jaw. This arms him with the widest jaw clearance and fiercest kype.

The second reason for this formation of the males' head is to aid in feeding. Large trout typically prey on food that can escape speedily. Equipped with protruding teeth and scissor jaws, the trout stands a better chance of securing a fast-moving meal. The male trout retains his exaggerated jaw throughout the year. And three months prior to spawning, the aggressive male adds slight growth to jaw and kype, extending the length of the jaw and size of the nub on the kype.

Female Trout

Female trout have less radically shaped heads and jaws. Unlike a male trout male, the female does not need additional dress for reproductive battle. The female has a more rounded, oval-shaped head and jaw. She doesn't have a kype. The jaw is normally the same length on the top as it is on the bottom. While large females don't have features as pronounced as the males, really large females also have a line of small sharp teeth which helps them obtain their food. To distinguish the female trout from the male you should look at the front part of the jaw. If the snout is rounded and without a kype, the fish is a female.

LENGTH AND GIRTH

Male Trout

While male trout have the potential for enormous girth, because the trout are generally more active and are in constant motion throughout the year, their body structure tends to be leaner. This is particularly true before and during spawning time. As in human males, this hyperactivity makes a male trout's body firm. Such active fish have a streamlined profile. Their bodies appear as one fit muscle.

Female Trout

Female trout have the capacity to really gain weight. While the males have taut hard bodies, the females tend to display broader width and distended bellies. Especially when they are in pre-spawn before they mate, they are large in weight with eggs, weighing more than other trout in the water. Their body structure is soft-bodied and less lean. This is partly because they are not wasting energy battling other females. When they are active, it's normally for shorter periods of time. They tend to lose less actual body weight before spawning.

Some of the largest trout I have seen have been female. I remember one special fish in a stream in upstate New York. I was walking up stream looking for the big one. It was one of those days where the lighting was off, due to the reflection of the white cotton clouds on the waters surface. I couldn't see more than four feet in front of me, and in these situations you have to move slow and really scan the water in front of you. If I walked at a fast pass, I would run the risk of spooking any trophy trout in sight.

I came across a side channel of water that was a good three and a half feet deep with an even-moving riffle current. I didn't think much of it because it was so narrow, so I was eager to move on. Just then I notice movement out of the corner of my eye. I dropped down on one knee then focused in on the area.

My first thought was, *Are you kidding me, there's no way a trout that big is in this small channel!* But once I got a clear view, I saw it was a monster. I estimated her size at 25 to 30 pounds. She was 40-plus inches long and at least a dozen inches between the eyes.

I soon realized with her flashing movement's this fish was in the act of spawning. If she wasn't on a spawning bed, I would have cast to her. Instead, I respected the ritual and realized that the future of a healthy population of trout starts with successful spawning. And looking at the size of this beauty, she was going to help produce some BIG numbers of wild trout. Just the thought that such an amazing fish inhabits accessible waters in a populated part of the world was enough to make my day in waders.

COLORATION AND MARKINGS

As with the formation of their heads, male and female trout display body markings and coloration that vary from each other. These manifestations change throughout the year.

Male Trout

Male trout generally have the brightest and boldest coloration. Some fish are so beautifully marked it looks as if someone painted its side lipstick red. The accentuated colors play a role for male trout during its life. A male rainbow, for example, is typically deep scarlet. On a few rare occasions I have had the privilege of landing male rainbows with two bold red stripes on their bodies—"double red sides," I call them. I have even caught large male trout so draped in colors that the bold red stripe was so wide, it reached from the lateral line to the bottom of the fish. The entire fish except its back was ruby red! There are two main reasons for these beautiful markings:

To show dominance. When in the water with other males, the larger the individual fish, the more color there normally is on its body. Small males see this as a warning sign.

To attract mates. Astonishingly bright male trout draw females to spawning water. I believe large painted males also make the attracted females feel less wary and safer. While bold colors serve their purpose in nature, it is also an excellent way for you to spot a giant trout.

Female Trout

Female trout are generally more subdued in color. But this is not always the case in water with an exceptionally large supply of protein as the food source—for example, freshwater scuds. Such a rich diet can alter the pigmentation and coloration of the resident trout, causing females to develop coloration nearly as bright and bold as the males. And they normally maintain heightened color throughout the year, not only during spawning season.

In most cases, while the female displays beautiful colors, she won't be quite as bold as the male, with colors highlighting her gill plate and running down the belly or lateral line. I personally think that these pastel-like shades covering a female trout are as beautiful as the vibrant colors lighting up the male. Less-flamboyant coloring protects the females by making them harder to see—and thus more elusive—in the water. Remember, the female is the attracted, not the attractor.

BEHAVIOR

Large trout are opportunistic feeders. They are habitually migratory, aggressive, and territorial when they are active. They are also smarter when compared to average or smaller trout—they simply have been around longer.

Wild trout especially are highly adaptable to changes in their environment. Generation after generation, the survivors successfully learn how to stay safe and most economically secure the highest source of protein available in any given water. The genetic code for toughness is passed on.

There is a difference in the behavior of male trout and female trout of any species, it is most noticeable when they are preparing to spawn. The reason is that leading up to spawning most fish that make themselves scarce the rest of the year are suddenly more active and visible. Often they have an "attitude," making them less concerned about the threats around them and more aggressive when feeding. For an alert angler, this is a good thing.

Male Trout

Large male trout appear first in advance of spawning season—spring for cutthroat, cuttbows, and rainbow trout; fall for brown, mackinaw, and brook trout. They are searching for water suitable for reproduction and, once they find it, their mission is to guard it until the females show up. You'll find that the very largest male trout are usually alone. They don't like competition. Not only are dominant male trout territorial, they are also highly aware of their surround-

This giant rainbow wasn't easy. I searched all day before I found the 15-pound female holding in a deep run. Her position forced me to adjust the weight on my leader to get my flies down to her.

ings, and know exactly where to go for cover the instant they feel threatened.

Because oversized male trout are exceptionally aggressive, they repeatedly charge and bite each other while fighting for territory. They continue this battle ritual until a female is attracted to the water and begins to cut a redd or spawning nest. The biggest male always has first rights and carefully guards his sexual prerogative through the entire spawning ritual, which can last days. This presents you and me with a fantastic opportunity to fish streamers. They'll hit the fly to kick the intruder the heck out. I've had some of my greatest fun with trout in such situations.

I like to call this "bugger time." When you can throw a Woolly Bugger into shallow riffles and watch the wake of a large male rushing to attack your fly—when this happens, boy, what a rush!

Don't worry about disrupting the sacred spawning process. The egg-laden female is not at risk. The female usually pays no attention to anything but her continuing task of excavating a clean, large redd through where oxygen-filled water flows freely. The male trout is the attack dog. He's the one chasing and grabbing your fly. And if you're lucky enough to catch and release the big guy—assuming you play him quickly so as not to overly exhaust him—he'll be none the worse for wear. Sit on the bank and watch the water. Before you know it, he'll be right back in there, by her side, dying to release his milt at the moment she releases her eggs.

Female Trout

The female trout's behavior is markedly less aggressive. While males are ever eager to battle for the best spawning water and the greatest number of mates, the largest females—while holding downstream in preparation for spawning or while actual-ly spawning—are seldom challenged by other females. Prior to the start of gravel excavation, in fact, they do not waste much energy at all. This keeps them and their ripening eggs healthy. They seek cover in deep water and migrate with other females only once the time is right for spawning. This is very similar to their activity during the rest of the season. They are often found with other females in a variety of water conditions.

A special point to remember: Female trout in shallow water are exceptionally wary of predators. I have found they require a stealthy, well-planned presentation. Don't rush anything. Take your time *before you make a single cast.* Think through your approach before you make your move. Come to think of it, this is not bad advice about approaching a female of any species.

MIGRATION PATTERNS

Travel is an important strategy in the life cycle of a trophy trout, whether the population to which he or she belongs is naturally migratory or generally resident in a particular river. The ability to migrate allows fish to leave a place when habitat conditions becomes less than desirable—when the water gets too warm, for example—and it also allows fish to move to a new location in search of food or mates. Long term, migration stacks the deck in favor of survival of their offspring; short term, moving around puts individual trout in a position to maximize their potential for converting calories into pounds.

The most important thing a large trout can do to ensure its survival is adjust readily to changing environments. Fish adjust by taking up residence in different waters at different times of year. I'll say this now: By far the best chance for you to catch a trophy trout is during the pre-spawn, and post-spawn weeks—when the trout have to adjust by moving into shallow water, and are more exposed to you, the angler. Don't forget it. It's the creed of any big-trout angler.

Because trophy trout are so effective at accomplishing this, it makes their migration patterns tolerable to the fish. By understanding the timing of and reason for the journey, you will be prepared to be at the right place at the right time to ensure your shot at a big one.

WHY BIG TROUT MIGRATE

There are many reasons why trophy trout migrate. The most obvious of course is the imperative to reproduce. This supersedes all animal instincts. But it doesn't stop there. In fact, large trout are known to travel the same distances they do to spawn for other reasons. Here is a short list why trophies migrate:

- Spawning (brought on by the daily cycle of sunlight and water temperatures)
- Food supply
- Fishing pressure

The most powerful stimulant arousing a trout to move—into a river system from a large body of water, or within a river system and up tributaries feeding that river—is to reproduce. The urge to spawn is hormonal, triggering them to travel in search of the right gravel. When hormones take over, nothing can stop the fish. The three primary factors sending them on their way are:

- Time of year
- Diurnal cycle of sunlight
- Water temperature

NOTE: These three variables act in linkage, like a chain reaction.

TIME OF YEAR

There are two principal seasons when most trout spawn. Cutthroat, cuttbow, and rainbow naturally do their thing in the

This spectacular female rainbow trout fell to my Mysis Shrimp fly. Her oval jaw and pastel colors were quite a sight after a hard day on the water. I wouldn't have had a chance without a fluorocarbon tippet.

spring. Browns, lake trout ("Mackinaw"), and brookies head for the red come autumn. This ancient schedule is the best shot you have at a trophy trout. The two spawning seasons are transitional periods during which fundamental changes occur in the temperature of air and water, length of day, and often in volume of water flow. All of these various changes within these two seasons play roles in the whereabouts of giant trout. The first is the so-called "diurnal" cycle of sunlight.

CYCLE OF SUNLIGHT

To simplify, the diurnal cycle refers to the hours of sunlight in a day. This plays a key role in causing trout to migrate. It is not as if the fish know the exact number of hours in a day. However, they react to what happens when days get longer in the spring and shorter in the fall.

There are two days per year when earth receives an identical amount of sunlight: the spring equinox in March and the autumnal equinox in September. Between

It's not every day you can get a monster rainbow to smile—I crawled on all fours to get into casting position without spooking him. Stealth is a vital part of a strategy for trophy trout.

the two are the winter and summer solstices. Following the winter solstice in December, the length of daylight hitting earth increases daily. Following the summer solstice in June, the length of daylight diminishes with each 24-hour revolution.

This cycle of sunlight directly affects trout. As winter wanes, days gradually grow longer. Sunlight grows stronger, causing air and water temperatures to warm, slowly at first and then accelerating as the weeks go by. As food becomes more abundant, the metabolism of trout increases. Months later, as summer comes to a close, the process reserves itself—less sunlight causes the river to chill and feeding to slacken. These seasonal fluctuations in temperature and daylight trigger the spawning migrations of trout.

WATER TEMPERATURE

Changes in temperature are a signal to the fish that the season is changing and the spawn is close. I will never forget the first year I was in upstate New York in search of trophy browns. The air temperatures that fall were incredibly warm, making me wonder if global warming is real. It's just not supposed to be that warm in October. I'm talking 75°Fahrenheit in the third week of the month!

My trip was planned for seven days of fishing, and fortunately I arrived two days before a cold spell. The first two days were slow. Temperatures were warm and slowly starting to drop. The night of the second day, thankfully, the temperatures dropped into the low 20s. The following day actually felt like fall with temperatures around 40 to 45°. By the afternoon of the third day the fish started coming in like freight trains, and the rest of the trip was a success with a constant flow of monster browns moving into the river. This experience underscored just how critical water temperatures are to

fishing success—one day the river was empty, the next day the pools were stacked with fish.

Where I do most of my fishing, trout in fresh water are most active in water temperatures generally ranging from 50 to 65°. This is a broad range of course and there are many local exceptions. Generally, in springtime the best trend for fishing is cold to warm; and in late summer or early fall, warm to cool. Atmospheric weather is the factor most influential in determining these trends. Tracking the weather on a daily basis will increase your chances of success. Whether a new front brings snow, rain or sun, a sudden change in weather can change the river. Depending on the situation, this can be either good or bad.

Several seasons ago in October—in my opinion, the single most productive month to catch a trophy trout—there was a warming trend that lasted almost three weeks. This caused water temperatures to remain unseasonably high and delayed the spawning run of big browns I was waiting for. The flows were high. All the conditions were right except for the desperately desired cooling water temperatures that colder fall days and nights normally bring. I prayed for snow.

Water temps for trout are different in various regions of the U.S. by a few degrees. Generally speaking, in the spring, rainbows, cuttbows, and cutthroat trout prefer water ranging from 42 to 50. In the fall, brown, Mackinaw, and brook trout prefer water from 45 to 55. While the degrees may change slightly for various water ways, these general temperatures discussed here are reliable.

WATER FLOWS

The last but not least reason causing large trout to migrate is water flow. Everything can be perfect for trout to spawn—good weather, perfect temperatures, and so on—and yet fish stay as lively as a doorknob. Before they move en mass, sometimes they stage up, waiting for the right water depth to start their journey. This is common on many tailwater drainages. The easier it is for large trout to migrate, the more numbers of large trout you'll see in various waterways.

The rise and fall of water flows also greatly affect water temperatures and can cause a fluctuation of as wide as several degrees in different waterways. So always check the flows for the areas you plan to pursue trout. Know what the baseline is. And be alert for a rise in water to draw the big ones in. The "right" water depth varies from river to river. Often it is linked to water temperature. My preference for fly fishing is water from two to four feet deep.

Keep in mind, too, that trout are looking for stretches of water attractive for spawning. The ideal substrate material typically consists of gravel measuring two to two and a half inches in diameter. The flow should be even and moderate. This combination provides the best conditions for the fertilized eggs to incubate and hatch. Some trout travel a short distance to spawn, while others travel many miles. How far they go depends on the quality of spawning habitat and competition for redd space. This is why large trout sometimes travel up improbably smaller tributaries, where they find just the right river bottom and water depth to spawn.

Although spawning is the main reason for trout to migrate, there are other reasons trout change addresses. The difference, when they are forced to move—by low water, for example, or exhausted forage—is they are not as eager to move as when sex is the motivation, and the timing of their movements is not as predictable.

FOOD SUPPLY

Aside from spawning, the greatest motivation for an animal to move is food—any food when the animal is starving, more food if he's getting some food but wants more, or he's developed a desire for tastier food.

Perhaps the most dramatic spectacle of resident trout swimming elsewhere for nutrition is in Alaska, where native rainbows eat the eggs and flesh of sockeye salmon entering shallow rivers by the millions from August through September. This run is so intense that the rivers turn into a sea of red. You literally have strain your eyes to visually identify a trout in such a mass of salmon. The immense concentrations of spawning salmon supply these impressive silvery rainbows with a substantial supply of protein necessary to maintain their size. A steady diet of sockeye eggs and flesh provides a protein-rich feast for the trout that no quantity of insects could equal. And boy do they get a rich supply. I have personally witnessed the river bottom turn into an orange cloud of eggs. There were so many egg's floating along the bottom, I couldn't get a trout to hit an imitation because they couldn't see them. It was like an intense caddis hatch, but they were eggs!

A lesser but regionally vital version of this carnage takes places each September in many Great Lakes streams hosting runs of transplanted chinook or king salmon. Large brown trout commonly travel upstream with the salmon to eat the eggs and the flesh before the browns themselves spawn later.

Investigate the runs of fish in your home waters to determine if there is a special food giant trout find irresistible.

PRESSURE

In addition to food, the second non-sexual reason fish migrate is protection from predators. This, by the way, includes the ultimate predator—pressure from anglers, particularly on many tailwater fisheries in various states.

There are some stretches of river below dams where the water is narrow and clear, and giant trout congregate. The word of catching trophy trout spreads quickly. Hordes of trophy-seekers and a mob atmosphere take over. This focused harassment forces the trout to less-pressured waters with less stress and movement from above.

I'll never forget the day my fly-designer friend John Barr caught this handsome brown in front of me: It had a six-inch chub sticking out of its mouth yet still took John's fly. Talk about being hungry!

It's not that the trout "know" there are a lot of anglers after them; it's the movement from all the activity that causes the fish to feel nervous and then at risk. Too much pressure makes them even more wary to predators.

A good example of this phenomenon is the tailwater below a dam. While rainbows often move freely throughout the public water below the dam to spawn during springtime, when swarms of people show up during the summer months the fish unfailingly retreat to the no-trespassing water downstream. They may also drop into the private water below.

So do your homework: Be mindful of the amount of pressure in any fishery as you hunt for giants, and try to get there early in the season. In bad weather this will often result in fewer people on the water and happy non-pressured fish. Happy trout are taking trout.

FEEDING BEHAVIORS

One of the things I love dearly about large trout is their willingness to eat. They never seem to get enough. Big fish seldom pass up a chance at a large protein-based mouthful. They're gluttons, plain and simple.

To hook most large fish, the magic trick is not so much your choice of fly but rather your presentation and cast—in other words, stealth. The trick is not to spook the fish.

Many anglers have concluded that big trout are difficult to catch because they are not as willing to take. Wrong. They are *more* willing to take.

The reason these fish are more willing than average-sized trout is because they are opportunistic feeders. Most large trout are willing to chomp on any item of food within their feeding lane, and they are willing to move to obtain a large protein-based food source if it becomes accessible. Large trout must eat constantly to achieve and maintain their size, devouring with relish all kinds of food other than predictable aquatic or terrestrial insects.

I was happily introduced to this occurrence of large trout filling up on a non-insect source of food on the Nak Nek River in Alaska. During the high season there, late August through September, when trophy trout are feeding on endless supplys of salmon eggs and flesh, my fishing buddies and I were so successful using egg patterns and flesh flies that it was hard to tie on anything else. The fishing was so good. But Don Mehean, owner of Nak Nek Anglers, was quick to show me how deadly mice patterns can be on the edge of the river's bank. When I first saw a monster rainbow come up and inhale the deer-hair mouse imitation off the surface of the water, my jaw just about hit the river.

The over-the-top experience gave my fishing vocabulary a whole new meaning to the term "dry fly."

This taught me that fully understanding the trout's diet—and never underestimating its boundaries—can lead to unexpected results. Growing trout generally shift their diet once they reach a mature length of 12 to 14 inches. Insects are no longer enough. The age of this transition time is around three years of age. At this time of the trout's life they will begin to prey on food rich in protein. Their newly expanded diet is likely to consist of:

- Baby trout (fry)
- Other fish
- Sculpins
- Crayfish
- Mice

Such food items supply the proteins required for a trout to become a trophy-sized specimen. Unlike many insects, these creatures possess the ability to escape from predators. Large trout must chase them down and many become highly skilled at locating and killing them.

In addition to large forage, other food sources of smaller individual size but larger in collective numbers inhabit many waters that hold trophy trout: scuds, mysis shrimp, sow bugs, cranefly larvae, and aquatic worms are good examples. While these crustaceans and aquatic-dwelling insects are not exceptionally large in size, they are rich in protein, and thus important components in the diet of a large trout.

AUTHOR'S TIP

Refer to Chapter 10 for additional information on favorite sources of food for trophy trout.

Depending on the river (how prolific and complex is the base of aquatic insect life), most trout change their foraging behavior when they are somewhere between 12 and 17 inches in length, when they begin to hunt down and prey on larger animals. This doesn't mean they give up bugs. They simply become more opportunistic, continuing to gobble up terrestrial and aquatic insects, crustaceans, and other water-based life where and when abundant.

Many large trout become ambush predators. They take over areas where they can key in on large prey while average-sized fish still feed selectively and exclusively on a diet of insects. Because large trout are opportunistic feeders, they are willing to eat in all conditions. Understanding what the trout's principal food supply is in your favorite river, and where this food is most abundant, is crucial to locating the most promising water to invest your angling hours.

I believe most large trout will not pass up a sunken fly when presented properly in their feeding zone—it is clearly the most productive technique. But don't limit your thinking. In most rivers there are occasional surprising opportunities to seduce a giant trout to take a top-water fly. While it is a fact that most trout consume most of their food below the surface (about 80 percent of their diet), and spend most of their time searching for food there, in the right situation and under the right environmental conditions, there are times when big fish feed on top. Brief springtime hatches of huge salmonflies in western rivers come to mind. Sometimes it's triggered by weather. Brown trout are known to zero in on grasshoppers blown into the river or hopping off the bank into the water through the course of a warm, windy fall afternoon.

When there's size and protein enough in seasonal floating food to entice real giants into expending energy, don't hesitate to try a few casts. You might end up enjoying some exciting top-water action. For a reference in understanding food trout are likely to key in on, I look for these things first: highest protein and quantity. Find the highest protein-based food source in waters where the desired food source is most abundant and you will almost always find large trout waiting for a hearty meal.

CHAPTER 2

When To Hunt For Giants

TIMING IS EVERYTHING—how many times have you heard that cliché? Well, when pursuing trophy trout, you had better believe it. Being there at the right time can turn an average day into a magical fishing experience. Being in the right spot on the right day *and at the right time* requires a serious investment—lot of hours spent paying your dues.

I have driven, rowed, paddled, climbed, hiked, and crawled in search of giant trout. And I have found that there are distinct windows of time throughout the year with prime openings for catching trophies. Such a window of opportunity can range from as wide as two months to as narrow two weeks during certain times of the year. With this in mind, investigating waters that hold big fish will give you a better chance of being there when the fishing is hot and when there are a good number of fish in the water.

Along with catching and landing a trout of a lifetime, spending hours searching for fish has taught me a great deal. It's a big part of the attraction of catching these elusive creatures. I enjoy this part of the hunt because it increases my ability to learn the behavior of big fish quickly, and adds dimension to my experiences with the many fine anglers with whom I have shared my experiences throughout the years. If catching large trout were easy and not challenging, it simply would not be as much fun.

There are two important variables when determining what time of year is best to hunt for trophies. You want to determine if the fish in the body of water are resident river trout, or migrating trout. Resident river trout are fish that reside in the river throughout the year—they rely on the source of food in the river for their main diet. Resident fish are accessible to you all year. Residents still travel upriver or down during certain times of the year, but you can determine this time frame easier because they are in an accessible fishing environment when they travel. By covering (investigating) water and fishing various locations, you will eventually learn the patterns and behaviors of the fish that live there full time.

Often the habitats that hold giant resident river trout have a unique food base high in protein and large in volume. For example, in Colorado there are three notable rivers with an abundance of Mysis shrimp that are jettisoned from bottom-released dams. These shrimp provide a quality protein source, which enables the trout to grow quickly and become very large in size. In Alaska, summertime brings huge runs of sockeye salmon, which attracts trophy trout that follow the salmon into rivers and feed on the super-abundance of eggs.

Once you identify a river's primary food source, your next step is to find out if there are certain times or water conditions that make it more readily available to the fish. This could be a rise in water flows, a hatch during the day, or forage released in the outflow from a dam. The point is to find out what the protein source is and where and when the fish feed heavily on it.

TIMING THE MIGRATION

Migrating trout are fish that reside in a

One of those moments for simply enjoying where you are and what you're doing. I love this sport.

reservoir, lake, or large body of water and travel into the river system during a certain time of the year. The amount of time they spend in the river is determined by their objective. These fish migrate to these waterways annually to spawn and retreat back to the body of water when they have completed their ritual. At other times they may move into flowing water in search of food. They stay and feed in this environment as long as the food source is abundant.

Another reason for trout to move is water flow. Often a rise in the flow of water in the river causes a fluctuation in temperature at the inlet of a reservoir. This triggers a reaction in the trout, drawing them upstream. A rise or fall in water temperature can also entice the fish to migrate. When fish come from a large body of water and migrate upriver, they sometimes travel great distances. It is not unusual for trout to travel three or more miles in a day. Knowing that fish are on the move, it is good strategy to cover a lot of water when you are hunting for giants, constantly visiting the river to search for them.

A trick I have used throughout the years to keep track of all this accumulated knowledge, while visiting many productive rivers, is my trusty log and journal. It's nothing fancy—just a simple notebook filled with tips and information from my journeys in search of trophy trout. But it contains gold.

My journal has been especially helpful in planning future trips. In looking forward to each new season, I often read back to remind myself what has worked for me in the past for specific species of trout in a wide range of waters. Take the time to start writing your own big-trout journal—believe me, it will help you more than you realize in piecing together the puzzle of knowing when, where, and what time. It won't be

long before you'll be mining your own gold.

It is helpful to identify which species of trout are more productive in a certain season. Some seasons are better than others for catching certain species. In the spring, the following trout migrate:

- Rainbow trout (*Oncorhynchus mykiss*)
- Cutthroat trout (*Oncorhynchus clarki*)

In the fall, they are:

- Brown trout (*Salmo trutta*)
- Brook trout (*Salvelinus fontinalis*)
- Lake ("Mackinaw") trout (*Alvelinus namaycush*)

UNDERSTANDING THE SPAWN

Probably the most common time for anglers throughout the world to fish for giant trout is during the season when a particular species spawns. During this time of year, otherwise reclusive fish are less wary of predators. They move into more accessible water. They are more visible. This is obviously a huge advantage for you in seeing and presenting your fly to a trophy.

As this season of high-hormonal influence approaches, the aggressive nature of the fish intensifies. The water they prefer is shallower than usual and this makes them easier to spot—the depth might be only one to two feet. Seeing a trout of exceptional size in such a confined environment gives new meaning to thrill-seeking sports. What an adrenaline rush! It is common to see fish during this time of year that normally are not in the river or, if they are, they are hidden. There are three stages during this time of year when the fish move around:

- Pre-spawn
- Spawn
- Post-spawn

BEFORE SPAWNING

This is the most productive time of year to hunt for trophy trout. The fish are fresh, very aggressive, and are more likely to take a fly. During this time the largest fish tend to move around and are active first. The males are often the first to appear in spawning water or migrate in search of suitable water. The male fish are extremely aggressive and territorial. They'll smash your flies. The largest males are found in shallow water waiting for spawning mates.

During the first couple of years when I focused on fishing for large trout, there were times when I caught large males regularly and other times when I didn't. It was hit or miss. When I found them in large numbers, though, they were always big and full of fight—they gave everything they had until they were in the net. I started realizing that there is a pattern or schedule the fish follow during their pre-spawn phase.

> ## AUTHOR'S TIP
>
> *Be sure to log all your time on the water, including the days the trout are not active or in the waterway. This will help you accurately determine why the trout aren't in, and give you a better idea of when you should be searching for giants on this water. I like to keep a journal so that I can compare notes from year to year.*

If you can get there early enough, you too will experience these aggressive beasts in their top form. I'm sure, like me, you will see the difference in size, power, and robustness of these fresh fish. Make a special point to be at the water during the pre-spawn.

Female trout arrive after the males, staging in deeper water and runs. They do this until conditions are right for them to spawn in the shallows. This pre-spawn stage is the best—and, in my opinion, most ethical—time to catch big female trout because they aren't on spawning beds. They are big and fat and not yet dropping eggs. They are willing to eat because they are not in spawning mode. The earlier you can find pre-spawn fish the better your success will be in finding the largest trout during this time of year.

SPAWNING

When most fish are in the spawning mode, they are not eating and are often times not willing to take a fly. I won't fish to spawning trout and it is important to let the fish spawn unstressed in hopes of a successful reproduction of that species in the water you are fishing. It is easy to see the fish in the water because the male and female are often found together on the spawning beds in shallow water. The amount of energy they expend is amazing.

Hooking and fighting actively spawning fish can exhaust and potentially kill them. The proper way to fly fish during these conditions is to concentrate on the deep runs below shallow water—or fish an area just behind a spawning area. This is where an egg pattern can produce great results. The females drop their eggs in large numbers, many of them getting washed downstream. These drifting eggs become a source of high-protein food for other fish. It is proper etiquette to let the fish do their thing and don't pull them off their spawning beds. Fish the area below and you will understand why "the tug is the drug."

AFTER SPAWNING

Post-spawn is the last part of the season when giant trout are found. Many of the bigger fish retreat to the water they held in before the spawn. Some fish stage in deeper runs. They start consuming large amounts of food to replenish the energy lost during

Jenn O'neal, the "Fishing Machine," put on a virtual clinic the day she landed this 14-pound giant. Our trip to New York together was one of the most fun fly-fishing adventures I've been on. Good job, babe.

the spawn. This gives you the advantage because this is the most productive time to entice these fish to take a fly. However, they are also more wary of predators because they are no longer obsessed with sex. This means you will find them in deep runs or water with a lot of cover.

Because of how much energy they spent during the spawn, the fish have lost some of their size, and it is better to pursue them later, once they have replenished pounds and energy. Loss of weight is especially apparent in female trout that earlier were full of eggs. Throughout the spawning cycle, these tired beauties can loose up to 30 percent of their total body weight.

Many anglers have a hard time holding back the urge to cast to fish on a spawning bed. I too have been there and felt the urge when seeing two huge fish exposed and highly visible in low, clear water. It's tempting. But then I started setting my rod down, taking a break, and watching this unique ritual performed by these awesome fish I have grown to love. By giving the fish a chance to reproduce and spread new life, you will ensure and help future generations of these trophies. So when you happen upon this spawning dance on your home stream this season, take the time to watch and enjoy. But do not disturb.

TIMING THE SEASONS

Without question, spring and fall are my absolute favorite seasons of the year for fishing.

Spring

Spring is when cutthroat, rainbow, and "cuttbow" trout spawn. I love this season because it's when a long winter is coming to an end and the trees, flowers, and creatures are full of life again. For the angler, this is the true start of a new beginning. It brings the promise that this will be the year for that fish of a lifetime, larger than any you've ever caught.

Fall

Fall is a magical time of year for hunting the big ones. I was born during this season, and each year I am thankful I am here to have these opportunities and to share some truly great moments in wonderful settings. Yes, summer days are pleasantly long and warm, but hope of cooler weather is always lurking in the back of my mind. Eventually, the temperatures drop and the first frost covers the ground. A new shade of color appears on the leaves. It's brown trout time! And this is my last chance to live up to the commitment I made to myself at the beginning of the year to land that "fish of a lifetime" bigger than the fall before.

During the fall, browns, brookies, and Mackinaw spawn. These times of year are when some of the largest trout are accessible to you because they come from waterways that give them the best cover and protection from predators. These areas can be large bodies of water such as lakes, reservoirs, and oceans. Or, for the resident river fish, these areas can be deep runs, under structure in the river or areas where they can hide and feed without pressure from above. For me, fall is my most productive fishing season.

Winter

Winter is when crowds on many waters disappear. If you fish near the mountains, powder days are better spent on the river rather than on a ski slope. The waters during this season are low and clear.

Few aquatic insects hatch now and food is scarce. Colder temperatures make the trout more lethargic than normal. Their metabolism decreases and they are not as willing to expend energy to obtain food. Making a good presentation to trout in these conditions is very important. These low, clear conditions do give you the advantage in spotting and finding fish not obtainable in high water.

During this largely dormant season, you are most likely to find a large trout holding in a secure environment offering both sanctuary and food. The best times to try your luck is in December, immediately after fall, and then again in March, in the days leading to spring. Some post-spawn fish are hanging around in early winter, and three months later in late winter, some pre-spawn trout make an appearance. Dress warmly, try to stay comfortable, and approach with caution to these wary but awesome trout.

Summer

Summer months are rich with aquatic life. Near-continuous and overlapping hatches provide a steady and robust source of food for trophy trout. This time of year, trophies are found in water that also holds resident river fish. The abundance of food entices even the largest trout to pluck a fly off the surface.

One of the key puzzles for the big-fish specialist to solve is which food source provides the highest levels of protein to the fish. Large trout are opportunistic feeders and must eat constantly to maintain their size. Although these giants are opportunists, they are normally not willing to expend an excessive amount of energy. Thus, most of their feeding occurs below the surface of the water. They don't often rise to the surface unless they are rewarded with an exceptional amount of protein (such as hoppers) or unless there are large quantities of a routine food source (e.g., large mayfly hatches).

A unique example of this is a trout eagerly waiting to smash a mouse that is frantically skittering across the water. I'll never forget my first experience fishing a mouse imitation. It was early August in Alaska on the Nak Nek River and on this day I was determined to nail fish on a mouse as I tied on the massive dry fly. I thought the trout that eats this is going to be massive. Well, after a skittering drift over a grassy area, the take was massive, but to my surprise, the trout was only a whopping 15 inches. This made me realize that some trout are trophies in spirit, but it may be a while for reality to set in.

Below the surface they can eat securely with good cover without expending as much energy. Because large trout are wary of predators, the best time to fish for them in the summer months is early morning or late afternoon, or during a large hatch while food supplies are plentiful. They can feed with less caution during these times because predators do not easily detect them.

Paying his dues in search of a trophy: Angus Drummond casting away in a blizzard, a frigid but productive day on the water. The lousy weather gives trout greater overhead security from natural predators.

This bright cutthroat was a welcome reward to my good friend Scottie Miller who persisted on a bright bluebird day. Scottie had to cast way upstream of this trout so he could get a drift without spooking it.

TIME OF DAY

Not only is showing up streamside at the right time of year critical, so is being there the right time of day. There are many advantages to being on the water at a certain times of day during different seasons. The most valuable thing you can learn from timing your trips to the river is to be there when the temperature is just right and the fish become more active, and also to be on the water at the time when the fish are less cautious of predators.

Spring

Springtime is an exciting time of year. This is when the rainbows, cutthroat, and cutbows prepare to spawn and become their most active. Timing during this season is important because the water and weather have been cold for so long during the winter. The fish become active when the water is warmed by nice weather. I prefer warm sunny weather that is consistent. Day by day, sunshine increases the water temperature. The fish become less lethargic and more active. This warming trend also gets the fish to move into new waters or moving about in their existing waterways.

There is a window of time between 1 and 5 o'clock when the fish are most active. The sun is at its highest point at noon and the warmest part of the day is during this period. Often the water temperature is warmed by two to three degrees. On many occasions, I have been on the river or covered a good section of water and had some success in the morning, then returned in the afternoon to the same water and seen fish that were not active earlier.

It's simple, if you time your trip when the fish are most likely to be active, you will experience better fishing.

Fall

Brown and brook trout spawn in the fall. This season is a transition from warmer weather to cooler weather. As the temperature drops, the fish become more active. I have found this to be the case in the early morning hours and in the late evening hours of the day, as well as on stormy, cloudy days.

Browns especially tend to travel great distances in the fall in pursuit of spawning grounds. Sunny warm weather can be a disadvantage during this time of year because the visibility in the water is better and the fish hide because they become wary of predators. I have found that cloud-covered days are the most productive days to pursue trophies during this time of year because the water temperature stays just right and does not get too warm. The fish feel safer and less wary and they stay exposed more throughout the day. This is the same reason why early morning and late afternoon on sunny days can be very productive. Timing it just right in this time of day and weather conditions in the fall can make for a successful trip in this colorful season.

WEATHER CONDITIONS

Weather conditions play a major role in fishing success. In fact, whether or not I leave my driveway is often dictated by the weather.

Stormy Weather

Cloudy, storm-filled days can be a challenge to spot fish, but also make the fish less wary. These days can produce great results. For one thing, there is considerably less pressure from anglers on the water. For another, the fish aren't as spooked by shadows or movement from above. This encourages them to move around the river more— and also makes it easier for you to present your fly and get numerous drifts to the fish while remaining undetected.

Visibility into the water is not as good in bad weather, so it is important to view the water as you are walking upstream. This will also help to prevent spooking fish in these conditions. Tread with caution. With all the pros and cons of fishing in bad weather, the thrill is being able to get close to the fish before presenting your fly. I remember countless opportunities in horrible conditions when I could literally reach out and poke the fish with the tip of my rod. It is not often you will get this up close and personal with a monster trout.

Here's a question: Have you ever seen a trout go belly-up due to shallow water? It's an interesting experience. I was fishing one fall in a small creek that was at widest, 10 feet. Thus far the season had been slow. But rain was finally raising the flows in the area. Because it was a driving rain, the water became stained, making it difficult to see in.

I was standing at the edge of a shallow riffle and casting into a deep trough in front of me. This was a perfect area for trophy trout to stage as they migrate up the creek. Or so I thought.

After fishing what seemed like only a few minutes, I witnessed something incredible.

A huge male brown trout that I estimated to be 15-plus pounds attempted to swim up the shallow riffles I was standing in. It was coming right at me! Because of its size it couldn't reach deep water. He then flopped on his side and let the trickle of water drift him back down to deeper water.

"How do you cast to a sideways trout?" I heard myself asking aloud. I was frozen in disbelief. That is definitely something you don't see every day on the water. I couldn't wait to run downstream and tell my fishing partners what happened. But I figured they would look at me as if I was nuts. So this is one for the vault. What a sight!

It's been my experience that in the fall particularly, bad weather frequently produces extraordinary results. The water cools to the perfect temperature and makes the fish—especially brown trout—less skittish. Browns are more independent and elusive than other species of trout. This season is when browns are on the move. The weather gives them the water conditions they need with less pressure from predators from above. This can help you become more effective with a fly rod.

Bluebird Weather

It is always a pleasure to be on the water when the weather is perfect and you couldn't be any more comfortable. The sun is shining and you can see clearly into the water. All this comfort can be an advantage. However, if it is easier for you to see the fish, it is easier for the fish to see you!

During days with sunshine and warm

temperatures, the fish normally become more active as the day drags on—assuming cool temperatures at night—and the water temperature rises, often two to four degrees throughout the day. While the fish are active, they are also on high alert for avian predators from above. In bright conditions, shadows, light reflections, and movement are more visible to the fish.

In fine weather, you can usually see into the water and a fair distance across river. Because the fish are wary, keep a low profile. Be observant. Pay close attention to the water as you work your way upstream. Early morning and late afternoon are good times during these conditions, because the sun is not directly above and the fish not as alarmed by movement. While these times can produce good results, you also lose some visibility into the water due to the reflection and angle of the sun. The trick to overcome this is to take care to position yourself with the sun at your back, keeping the sun and glare out of your face.

Next time you are on the water in wonderful summer weather and you spy a trophy trout, before you move a single move, stop and think carefully about the best approach.

There is nothing more exciting than seeing the magnificent red stripe of a 16-pound shrimp-fed rainbow in crystal water. I'm getting all worked up just thinking about it. I set my hook to the white of his mouth.

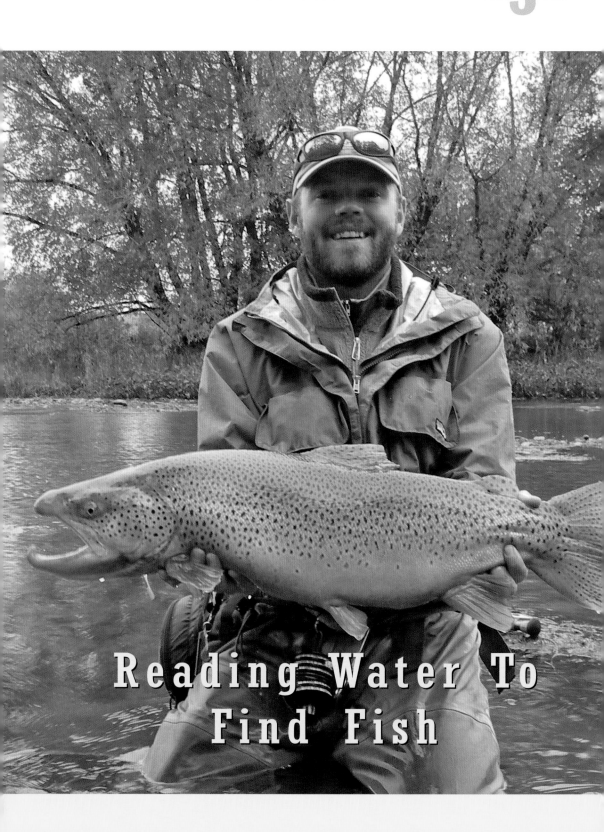

CHAPTER 3

Reading Water To Find Fish

WHEN I FIRST STARTED FLY FISHING, one of the huge breakthroughs that immediately increased my success was coming to understand that not all parts of the river are the same. The trout were in some spots, but not in others. This came as a revelation.

I see this all the time. I drive up to the river bank and start gearing up. Then I see the angler next to me start eyeing me while I put my waders on. Before I know it he's making a mad dash to his favorite run with his waders half on, his right boot untied, and his hat crooked. I always chuckle—little does he know I'm not in a race with him. My strategy is to hike all day, leading far away from him, covering stretches of the river where I think fish are holding.

It's easy for an angler to get content with one area of water where he or she has caught fish on previous trips. Don't fall into this trap. You're cutting yourself short by missing out on other potentially good water. No matter how experienced, we should all be open to learning something about even a familiar river, but certainly new water.

I point out to my clients after they land a trophy that they did so in between other anglers' fishing "their" favorite holes. This demonstrates that being able to read water not only opens your eyes to new water; it opens up areas with less traffic from other anglers.

I'm sure many other anglers, and not only beginners, share the same overwhelming feeling when fishing a new piece of water—*where should I focus my attention for my best shot at hooking up?*

This is when and where the universal ability to instinctively find water that holds fish places you ahead of the pack. Before you can sight fish, it is necessary to find water where the fish are. Basic but true. When "reading water" to find fish, you are essentially scanning sections of water where you think trout are holding, and making an educated guess. Many variables come into

play when trying to be effective with this method. I apply five quick measures to a stretch of water that I think might be holding fish:

- Security and cover
- Food supply
- Water flow
- Oxygen level
- Water temperature

Let's discuss why these five variables are important and why the fish rely on them for survival.

SECURITY AND COVER

Throughout the life of a trout, probably the most frightening predators are birds of prey—everything from mergansers to kingfishers to herons. These predators-from-above make fish wary of any movement, shadow, or reflection of light overhead. Every stream also breeds predators that live side-by-side underwater with the trout, and would eat the trout given half a chance. Understanding the trout's natural enemies—and where fish hold in a river pressure-free to avoid ending up in one's belly—is something you should consider when reading water.

Naturally camouflaged brown trout are the most difficult to spot. It's as if they melt into the river bottom. When you're not sure if it's a fish, pause and watch the spot for even the slightest sign of movement.

There are many areas where trout hide to feel secure. Some of these hideaways are surprising. It's hard to imagine a trout hiding in some. I've encountered some of the largest trout in rivers lying right out in the open, visible to me and anything else that might wish it harm. When the fish spooked, it seemed to disappear like magic. When a big trout vanishes, here are some common places it could be hiding:

Water Breaks: Areas where there is a break in the water or a disturbance on the surface of the water. These often distort the image in the water, making it difficult to obtain a clear visual of the fish.

Deep Runs, Pocket Water, and Pools: These are areas where the trout can use the depth of the water to their advantage, making them difficult to see. Often times the color of this deeper water makes even the brightest of markings on a trout disappear.

Structure: Trout often hold near structure in the water. These areas may consist of undercuts on the riverbank and under rocks, overhangs, trees, or logs. These structures allow the trout to hide with total cover and security.

Now let's look at the factors related to where the trout may be holding.

FOOD SUPPLY

We know that trout don't waste energy when foraging. When possible, they are downright lazy eaters. I like to tell my clients imagine eating a Twinkie every three seconds for the rest of your life. And the fatter you get, the more popular you become. Generally speaking, that's what happens with trophy trout. They hold in water that's not too forceful and where the current washes food right into their mouths—a feeding lane.

Trophy trout are the exception, notably before spawning when they are exceptionally aggressive. Then you can trick them into taking a baitfish, crayfish, or large-insect imitation. But you're still fishing the readable water where they routinely obtain most of their food. When looking for these chow lines, you should focus on flow.

WATER FLOW

Trophy trout are not only larger but also stronger than most trout. In moderate flows, they have a greater ability to hold where the speed of the current accelerates and carries a concentrated quantity of food around or through a relatively narrow funnel. This might be fast water around structure—often referred to as seams—shallow gravel runs that cause fast riffled water, runs or pools where the water gets deep fast due to a drop off point from shallow water above, and eddies or side current of a normal flow of water.

For many waterways in the U.S. there is always a chance at the water levels fluctuating up or down, especially in the spring or fall and in tailwaters below dams. Water flow is measured in cubic feet per second (cfs). In fact, some waterways have such significant flow that they are measured in units, each unit equals 350 cfs. For example, rivers in Missouri measure in such units and have sirens that sound before they release water from the dam. In addition, depending on the season of the year, other factors can cause the water to fluctuate, such as runoff, water demand, droughts, lack of water, snow, rain, ice, etc.

Keep in mind that all trout streams are subject to drastic flow fluctuations which change the water where the trout holds. There is time after a fluctuation in water flow that trophy trout need to adjust and find new resting water they find comfortable.

It is also important to remember that the area of water where the flow is the strongest isn't normally where the fish are holding. Rather, it is on the edge of this fast water. So positioned, the fish is not fighting the current to obtain its food—it's letting the current deliver the food.

Imagine these areas as a cushion within the water were trout can kick back as you or I might on our favorite recliner in front of the tube munching on popcorn. These sections let the trout eat undisturbed and free from harassment. If trout could talk I'm sure their response in these areas would be "What a life." You should keep this information in the back of your mind when looking over a stretch of water for the first time.

OXYGEN

Knowing where there is a good supply of oxygen in the water will help you find more fish. Most anglers ignore this factor when reading water, but it is crucial in keeping the trout healthy. And large trout particularly need a constant supply of well-oxygenated water streaming through their systems. There are four major occurrences in rivers that supply good oxygen to the fish.

AUTHOR'S TIP

In rivers where the flows fluctuate—predictably or erratically—the trout move around in response to current flows. For example, while the water is rising, trout tend to move into shallow-water areas where they couldn't hold before so that they don't have to battle the current. When the flows decrease, they tend to retreat to deeper water to find cover. Look for areas that provide cover, plenty of oxygen, and an abundant food supply. If you are fishing a river with fluctuating flows, you should adjust by evaluating the current conditions, and look for those ideal spots where fish are inclined to hold. Areas that hold fish when the flows are high are not likely to hold fish when the flows are low, and vice versa. Fish are required to adjust to fluctuating flows. To successfully hook them, you need to adjust as well.

COOLER WATER

Trout prefer cool water because cool water contains higher levels of dissolved oxygen. Also, the cooler the water, the less oxygen a trout requires—a double benefit. This is a huge factor in why cold water released from the bottom of a dam, when mixed with oxygen, often supports extraordinary populations of quality trout. This also applies to deeper runs and pools. When trout are in a healthy, cool environment, they stay active and eat more. When they eat, they grow.

AERATED WATER

Turbulent riffles are attractive areas for trout to hold in. The water is often created flowing off rocks on the bottom of the river. And trout in these conditions have a short window to commit to taking what appears to be a tasty bit floating by. The advantage goes to the angler, because the fish cannot investigate your fly for a long period of time. It's a fleeting temptation. The good news is that more than small fish like it here. This bubbly turbulent water is excellent habitat for trophies.

WATER OFF STRUCTURE

Physics dictates that a given volume of water accelerates in speed when forced around or above structure. This produces turbulent water, which in turn produces more oxygen in this area, allowing the fish to feed comfortably. There is nothing more exciting than watching a 10-plus-pound trout turn sideways in shallow water with its mouth open as big as a gallon bucket as it takes your fly. This is the heart-pumping visual you'll see when fishing shallow, well-aerated water. I am always optimistic when I find trophies in shallow water because I know my odds are good that the trout is comfortable—and most of the time willing to take my fly.

WATER TEMPERATURES

Water temperature is a critical component when it comes to trout activity, insect hatches, spawning activity, and health of a fishery. Obviously, the temperature varies markedly depending on the season.

During the Spring

Water temperature in the spring is especially vital when trying to locate trophy rainbow, because they are preparing to spawn. Warming water often triggers fish to move into new water (for example, from a reservoir or lake to an adjoining river) or to move around in their resident water.

I remember a good example of how important temperature is at this time of year. It was the middle of February and we were experiencing a warming trend that lasted just over two weeks. This is uncommon for this time of year. Air temperatures each day reached 60°F. I couldn't believe it. It felt as if Colorado had decided to skip spring and dive directly into the summer. It certainly did not feel like mid-winter.

Because of the unseasonably balmy weather, I decided to take a trip to a local stream to see if there was anything going on. I was excited to get on the water because I knew that with warming air temperature comes warming water—which equals huge trout on the move. Plus the earlier you find these migrating giants the fatter they are. They simply haven't used any energy yet.

AUTHOR'S TIP

Start a log of water temperature when you're on the water. No need to take a river's temperature when the trout aren't in. Take it when the fishing is hot—this will give you the perfect starting point in knowing what temperatures they prefer. Then every season to follow you'll have your own personal gauge telling you when the water is just right for the trophies.

When I arrived streamside, I was shocked by the color of the water. The snow was melting so fast the deep runs turned into pockets of pea soup. I had been in this situation before on other waters, and knew

What a cool image of a recently released trophy brown trout back and swimming in its natural habitat.

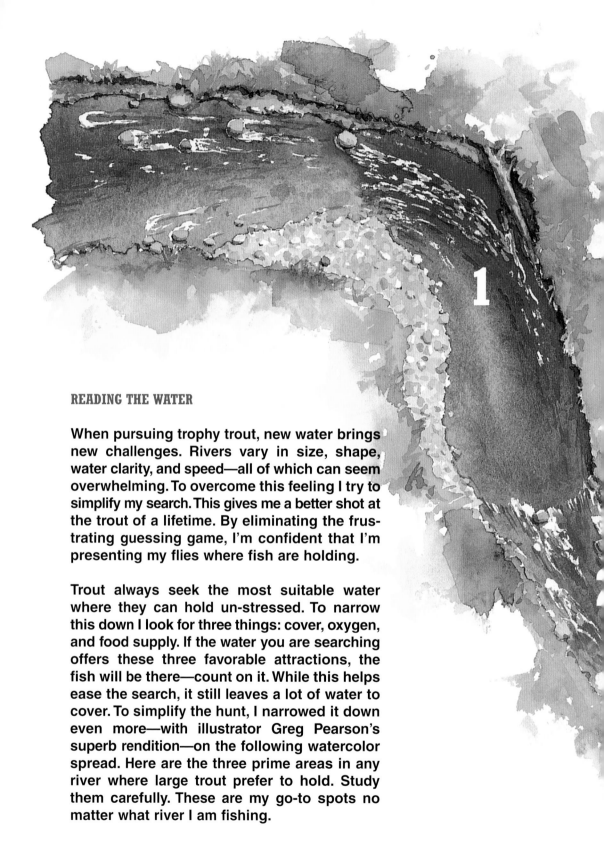

1

READING THE WATER

When pursuing trophy trout, new water brings new challenges. Rivers vary in size, shape, water clarity, and speed—all of which can seem overwhelming. To overcome this feeling I try to simplify my search. This gives me a better shot at the trout of a lifetime. By eliminating the frustrating guessing game, I'm confident that I'm presenting my flies where fish are holding.

Trout always seek the most suitable water where they can hold un-stressed. To narrow this down I look for three things: cover, oxygen, and food supply. If the water you are searching offers these three favorable attractions, the fish will be there—count on it. While this helps ease the search, it still leaves a lot of water to cover. To simplify the hunt, I narrowed it down even more—with illustrator Greg Pearson's superb rendition—on the following watercolor spread. Here are the three prime areas in any river where large trout prefer to hold. Study them carefully. These are my go-to spots no matter what river I am fishing.

DEEP RUNS:

In the fall brown trout migrate up from large bodies of water to spawn. When these fresh fish first enter the river they hold in deep runs in order to gain strength and replenish food supply before continuing their migration.

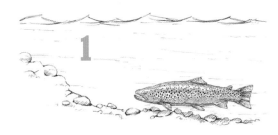

RIFFLED RUNS:

Riffled runs are essential for a trout's food supply, health, and well being. These areas often hold the largest trout within a waterway and allow you the best presentation. Without question some of my favorite water to fish.

IN FRONT OF ROCKS:

In most rivers trophy trout will hold in front of large boulders or rocks. This area creates a cushion of non-turbulent water where the trout can feed without expending much energy. This is one of my favorite target areas when hunting trophy trout.

See the raging rapids behind me? I came up close and personal with that current fighting this rainbow. It was all worth it, though, when I was able to keep my limbs intact and get a shot of this 12-pounder.

that even if the water looks unfishable, it pays to give it a shot—you might be surprised what's lurking below. So I did just that, starting my journey downstream.

The first thing I noticed was the runs that were normally four to five feet deep were now seven to 10 feet deep. Because the ice was still lining the rivers edge the water runs were compressed with faster current.

Ideal staging water, I thought to myself. Deeper runs and better cover from diminished water clarity—I couldn't wait to toss my flies in!

Once I found a run with suitable length to get an extended drift I was shocked: The river was *loaded* with monster trout. I have to admit there is something very intense about fishing water you can't see into, loaded with big trout, and the real question is how big is big? It's like mining for gold you

can't see but know is there. What a rush!

After spending the day on the water I ended up landing an absolute "pig" rainbow measuring 31 inches and scaling at 12 pounds. The next time I feel a warming trend in springtime, you know where I'll be.

Compared with other seasons, I've found spring the most difficult to predict when fish will be active and move into the areas I'm hoping to encounter them. Their movements are greatly influenced by the unpredictable weather during these months. Balmy temperatures can turn frigid in a matter of hours. When you are trying to determine the correct temperatures for rainbow and cutthroat trout, keep in mind that any warm weather can cause the water temperature to increase. This in turn can trigger the fish to move, even as early as late January or early February. The optimal temperature for rainbows and cutthroats during this time of year are generally 42° up to low 50s.

Start early when hunting for giants in the spring and keep detailed records of the weather and water temperature each time you go out. This will help you determine patterns in the activity of big trout. Even though this time of year can be bone-chilling cold, the adrenaline rush of landing your trophy can heat things up quickly.

During the Summer

Summer is the peak season for aquatic insect activity—and thus for trout activity. Water temperatures are pretty close to ideal and metabolism is at its highest. Small fish are growing and large fish are on the prowl.

I thoroughly enjoy fishing for trophies during these conditions because the trout are not distracted by anything other than feeding. For you and me, this means game on.

Fisheries created or augmented by water releases from dams maintain cool water at optimal temperatures during even the hottest months of summer. In most parts of the country, these trout-hospitable temperatures generally range from 55° to 65°F.

Unregulated freestone rivers are more susceptible to warming water and evaporation. It's a double whammy: Fish require more oxygen and there's less of it. This prompts the fish to seek spring seeps and faster-moving currents carrying increased oxygen, but at a cost—the fish must expend

This 10-pound brown Jim Brodie is holding up took on literally his last cast of the day. What an ending to a great outing on pressured water—way to go! Seconds later Jim proudly released his prize.

more energy. While freestone streams can produce large trout, they are generally more productive earlier and later in the day when temperatures are cooler and more comfortable for trout and their prey. When your stream thermometer reads 70° or higher, fish start shutting down. They are at risk of growing lethargic and stressed out.

The next time you are planning a summer trip to pursue a trophy trout, pick your river accordingly.

Without a doubt, I prefer to sight fish over any other style of fly fishing. My guess is that's the way you want to catch your trout of a lifetime, too. But to succeed you first need to know where to look. Following these strategies and techniques will help you become better at finding fish, knowing where to sight fish, and understand the behavior of big trout.

During the Fall

In fall the opposite happens. From September through October, the weather cools down, and this eventually drops the water temperatures to desired levels for brown trout, brook trout, and Mackinaw to begin their spawning rituals. Because the water has been warm all summer, you should plan your first trips when you are confident water temperatures are coolest—early morning, late afternoon, and overcast days.

Countless times I have been on the water and not turned a fish early in my fishing. When most anglers reel in for the day, I stick around. When a storm moves in that afternoon or late in the evening before dusk, big browns often come out of their hiding spots—it's amazing where these bruisers can hide and how they seem to appear from out of nowhere! This is when I have landed most of my large trout, especially browns. But of course if you see lightning crashing down, run like hell. Your graphite rod makes a pretty fair conductor

of electricity—at least that's the hypothesis. I for one don't want to test it.

The optimal temperatures for brown trout during the fall are generally 45° to 55°F. For Mackinaw and brook trout, the low to mid-40s are generally best.

Brown trout are migratory and travel great distances this time of year searching for spawning water. I frequently walk parallel distances following them. Be sure to eat your Wheaties. Big browns are known to travel three miles or longer in a day. Because they swim so far, they begin to move about and enter spawning tributaries as early as September and as late as December. Have your walking boots on. Get out there early and stay late. And remember that stormy days can be magical.

During the Winter

Someone I fish with in the winter is bound to be wearing felt-soled boots. While the felt is excellent for traction on mossy rocks in the water, on snow-piled banks anglers get a quick taste of life in high heels on an icy city street. Diabolically, layers of snow continue to stick to the bottom of your boots. By the end of the day you look like one of those people in the old V8 commercial tilted forward at a 45-degree angle: "What a trip."

AUTHOR'S TIP

Water flows are normally lowest during the winter. Sun shining on the shallows heats up faster. That's where you are likely to spot a fish.

Water temperatures are lowest in winter. Trout metabolism slows, sometimes to practically nothing. Feeding slows down.

Because fish are seldom willing to move much at all, you must present your fly discretely to them. It also must be spot-on accurate. On warm, sunny days the temperature might increase by a few degrees and at least temporarily awakening the hibernating fish. Hit the warming trends to find fish that might be in a sudden mood to eat.

The standout catch of the day: I was stunned when Eric Mondragon lifted this unreal brook trout out of the water. The amazing colors pop against the snowy backdrop yet in the water it was nearly undetectable.

Sighting Fish

WE ALL KNOW THE EXCITEMENT and thrill of seeing a trout sip a dry fly off the surface of a pool. It's the visual aspect of this fishing that makes it so exciting. I have discovered that "visual nymphing," provides a subsurface rush that has drawn me to become even more passionate about catching trophy trout. It also made me realize that the challenge of catching these giants is as much a visual game as any style of fly fishing

You are hunting or stalking the trout. Not only is this a thrill-seeking way to catch trophy trout, it has helped me better understand these elusive creatures. I have been tempted at times to pinch myself to believe what I was seeing is real. Some of these trout just look too big to inhabit the water they are lying in. That's a reality check. By learning and understanding the techniques in this chapter, hooking into that trophy will no longer be the chance of a lifetime. It will become a lifetime of chances.

Spotting fish is a learned technique and is possibly the most important ability in the challenge of catching a trophy. Spotting fish is easier on some days than others due to weather conditions—cloud cover and wind—and also based on strength of flow and clarity of the river. Being effective at sighting fish in various weather and water takes practice. It takes a special ability to scan the water and learn how to identify the fish. It is difficult to be comfortable looking through the surface of the water because of the distractions of glare.

A pair of quality polarized sunglasses is worth the investment, especially when hunting for trophies on days when the conditions are difficult. It is nearly impossible to accurately sight trout without using polarized sunglasses.

Sighting a fish in the water is not only a thrill, but seeing a large trout take your fly provides an adrenaline rush, as well as providing you a visual of when to set the hook and to observe what the fish does in the first few seconds of being hooked. Having a visual on the trout when it takes your fly

dramatically increases your ability to make a good hook set and usually prevents you from foul hooking the fish.

> ### AUTHOR'S TIP
>
> *The trick is to scan with unfocused eyes, and then focus in on what you think is a trout. This will allow you to see into a larger body of water rather than constantly focusing on specific objects, which will eventually strain your eyes and cause you to focus in on smaller areas of the river.*

During my first few years of pursuing large trout I learned quickly that in most situations, looking for the fish's reaction as my cue to set the hook is the best indicator. There are times when the trout takes the fly that its reaction may be very subtle and hard to detect. But because the trout are so damn big, when they move slightly or open their mouth, it automatically becomes an aggressive movement. If you have not already practiced relying on the trout itself as your indicator, I strongly recommend it.

If the conditions are exceptionally difficult due to weather or water clarity, this could require you to look for shadows, silhouettes, colors, or shapes in the water. This chapter will discuss what to look for when scanning the water, how to sight fish in low-light and bright-light conditions,

how to find "windows" or "viewing lanes," sighting fish in turbulent, choppy waters, and, if fishing with a companion, how the "buddy system" is used for spotting fish.

WHAT TO LOOK FOR

When spotting fish in the water, the most ideal situation is to get a detailed view of the fish and see all of its actions and movements. This is not always possible. When you are scanning the water to locate fish, the first and most important thing to

The white of a trout's mouth—exactly what I see through my polarized sunglasses when a fish feeds.

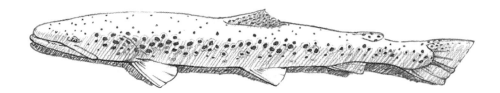

It's not often the angler sees a detailed image of trophy in the water. This situation is rare and can be intimidating because the risk is great that the trout will see you and spook. Use a stealthy approach, and rely on keeping a keen eye on the trout's jaw to tell you when to set the hook.

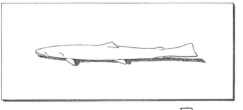

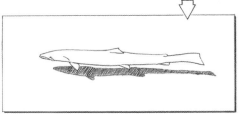

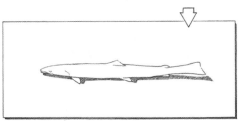

One of the most reliable ways to determine if you are looking at a trout in the river is detecting the natural movements made by the fish. An up-and-down movement is common when trout are feeding in deep water where the food is drifting downstream at different water depths. This causes the giant to suspend itself periodically. Finding a trout in this motion is a good indication that it's actively feeding.

understand is what colors and shapes to look for.

Often the first thing I see is the silhouette of the trout—its shape and shadowed outline. When you spot a silhouette you think is a fish, the next step is to watch for movement, which will determine if the silhouette in the water actually is a fish. Look for any natural movements made by a trout such as sideways swaying, tail or fin moves, and upward or downward motion.

By watching carefully for micro-movement, you'll learn to decipher if what you are seeing is a fish or actually some structure in the river. There are few more debilitating experiences in fly fishing than making a half dozen pin-point casts to what

One of my secrets for finding large trout in bright-light conditions is the shadow on the river bottom. On sun-filled days, their huge bodies cast shadows on the river bottom, giving away their locations. The bigger the fish, the larger the shadow. This is exceptionally helpful when hunting giants.

your pumping heart tells you is going to be the fish of the day, only to realize it's a log that looks as if it were carved to look like a trout. Trust me, I've been there.

When looking for trophies, another common technique is to look for markings and coloration. Because the best time of the year to hunt for trophies is before they spawn, the trout are conveniently marked with bright and elaborate colors, making them easier to spot in the water. Here are some examples of their coloration and markings:

- The red side and gill plate of a rainbow trout.
- The orange belly, fins, and gill plate of a cutthroat trout.
- Leopard spots and the yellow/orange belly of a brown trout.

If the conditions or water quality makes seeing colors and silhouettes difficult, there are a couple of other ways to get a visual on the fish. The first is to look for shadows of the fish on the bottom of the river. When you spot a shadow, pause and focus on the shape and watch for movement (as discussed previously). This method is effective in bright sunny conditions and in multi-colored river bottom areas. When fishing in lower light conditions, look for white in the river, which is often the inside of a fish's mouth, as this can be a dead giveaway.

MY LUCKY DAY

I remember one day in particular in late October when I was in pursuit of trophy brown trout, I arrived at the river and all was well. The water flows had remained steady for several days before I arrived and the water clarity was good. There was dark cloud cover above and it didn't look like there was going to be sun peaking through any time soon—perfect brown trout fishing conditions. Boy, was my luck about to change.

About two hours after arriving I noticed some debris floating downstream, and soon after the water turned to a dingy tea color. My visibility was now only two feet below the surface at most. I thought to myself: *I am screwed. There is no way I can see a fish in this.* So I started walking the river back to my vehicle. About 100 yards downstream, I noticed a couple of wakes shoot out from the bank. I stopped and scanned the water where I thought the fish stopped.

At first I couldn't see anything, but as I stared into the area I noticed a slight movement at what looked to be the tails of two brown trout. And, sure enough, when casting above the area and drifting through my effort paid off. I proceeded to look for this same visual movement of the trout's tails for the remainder of the day, and ended up with terrific results. In fact, this was one of my most productive days ever hunting browns in the fall.

This goes to show that even in the worst of conditions, there is always the possibility of still being able to see the fish. Once you have an understanding of what to look for in the water, you simply adjust to the unfolding and frequently uncertain weather.

SPOTTING FISH IN TOUGH CONDITIONS

The ability to adapt to difficult conditions on the water can make you more successful when stalking large trout. Probably the most challenging part of sighting fish is glare on the surface of the water. Glare reduces the angler's visibility into the water and makes it harder to find fish. Glare is the reflection of light off the water's surface; it resembles a mirror reflecting the light from above. The sources are many: bright sunlight, white clouds covering the sky, reflection of the sun off snow, sunrises, and sunsets.

Low-Light Conditions

Low light normally makes seeing fish easier because glare off the water is

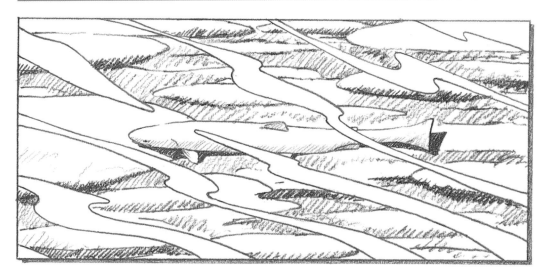

One of my favorite areas to target trophy trout on a river is a riffled run. These areas provide the fish secure cover from the disturbance on the surface—where nearly all their deadly predators have come from all their lives—and also a constant supply of food in bug-rich water. While big trout are comfortable here, they are often very difficult to see because of the obscuring chop on the water. In these situations, rely on the silhouette outline of the fish's body. This is achieved by scanning the river bottom with unfocused eyes.

Notice how the overall color of this trout's body blends into the river bottom? Only the red stripe on its side and gill plate looks out of place. Sometimes color is a helpful tool for spotting holding fish.

This brown looked like an orange alligator—easy to see but getting this guy in the net was another story.

reduced. This enhances your visibility into the water. Among the best times to fish during periods of low light are early in the morning just before sunrise, or late in the afternoon after the sun has started to set. You also have the advantage of the fish being less wary because they cannot see the threat of predators from above.

On cloud-covered days, the best situation is a dark sky. When a storm moves in and the sky is dark, the color on the water takes on the dark reflection of the sky, reducing the glare significantly, and allowing you to better spot the fish in the water. If the clouds covering the sky are white or light in color, the reflection on the water is bright, causing glare and making it difficult to see the fish. In this situation you have only small areas in front of you to see the fish. Scan the area thoroughly and move to either side of the stream to improve your visibility. This will allow you to view more water in a smaller area. Remember in low light, you have the advantage of the fish being less "spooky" because their visibility is reduced and you don't cast shadows on the water.

Bright-Light Conditions

Fishing in bright sun can be an advantage as well as a problem. The challenge is that the reflection and glare off the surface is extreme, making it difficult to spot trout. At the same time, the trout are easier to spook because they see well. The way to overcome this is to find a viewing lane in the river. The best way to find a viewing lane is to position yourself with the sun at your back. (More later about this critical strategy.)

Putting yourself in this position early in the morning and late in the afternoon allows the reflection off the water to be aimed at the opposite side of the river. It keeps the sun's rays out of your eyes, allowing you to see clearly into the viewing lane in front of you. Using the lane to your advantage

and covering water by looking in these sections of river helps you spot more fish and keeps you from missing fish in the water.

The advantage of bright light is your ability to see into the water at high noon. The sun is not at an angle and the glare off the water is reduced. This allows you to see into the river clearly. Midday hours are some of the most productive in bright-light conditions. While it is easier for the angler to see into the water, it is also easier for the fish to see you.

Be cautious. Observe carefully and cover the water thoroughly. And try to spot the fish from a good distance. This allows you to put yourself in the best position to cast to the fish without spooking it. There have been times when I have crawled on my belly to the edge of the river to avoid spooking a fish. While this might seem extreme or even silly, the end result of catching the huge trout you are sneaking up on will give you the last laugh.

WINDOWS OF OPPORTUNITY

When I first started pursuing trophy trout seriously, I found fish on just about every trip, but I usually spooked them because they saw me first. This was a problem. (I also suspected I was spooking other fish that I never saw.) So I devised a strategy of zeroing in on areas in the river with the highest visibility.

I wanted to see everything in the water. After a while, I realized that in almost any reasonable weather and stream flow there are windows of opportunity. These windows consist of:
- Viewing lanes
- Slick-water windows in turbulent waters
- River bottom
- The buddy system
- Viewing Lanes

A viewing lane is the most effective way

to find trout. What I call a "viewing lane" is a section of water upstream, downstream, or in front of the angler that allows you to see into the water without glare or reflection of color on the surface of the river.

This lane is typically four to eight feet wide. Its length can stretch from five feet in front of the angler to the other side of the river. The trick is to position yourself on one side of the river until you find the largest and clearest lane. If you get to the water on a sunny day, don't fret. Walk up to the edge of the river and look upstream and down. You'll quickly understand what a viewing lane is—it's the patch of water where there is no glare. Now follow this glare-free zone without taking your eyes off it. Once you find a good viewing lane, use it as your window into the water to scan for signs of a trophy. This allows you to approach the fish from behind and helps avoid spooking it.

When searching for fish, look over the entire lane in front of you before walking

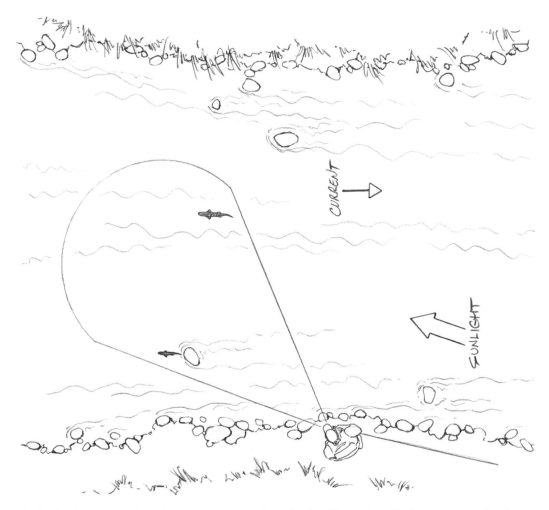

A viewing lane is a section of water you can see into clearly without glare. The lane can span five feet in front of you—or all the way across the river. It can be positioned upstream, downstream, or directly in front. To obtain the best visibility, find the lane with the sun at your back or directly above you. This is the key to sighting large trout. The trick is to be able to scan the lane at your walking speed, which allows you to cover the river quickly. If you spook a fish, you can watch it and wait for it to settle down and start feeding again. This is the most effective tactical tool I use for finding monster trout.

upstream until you have examined all the water. If the viewing lane is positioned downstream from you, keep a low profile and slow down your pace. Thoroughly cover the water—this helps keep the fish from detecting you. Once you have located a fish in a lane angled downstream, remember the area the fish is in and reposition yourself parallel to, or at a downward angle from the fish before you make your presen-

tation, again avoiding spooking the fish.

By understanding viewing lanes when hunting trophies, you increase your chance of seeing the fish before it sees you—the first step toward hooking the trout of a lifetime.

SLICK-WATER WINDOWS IN TURBULENT WATERS

Large trout hold in turbulent or choppy water because the break in the current gives

Big trout have an uncanny instinct to head for cover during battle. Four minutes, one log jam, two rock weirs, and a 100-yard dash downstream I landed this 10-pound brown. I was breathless. What a fight.

them cover and makes them less vulnerable to predators from above. This is a huge advantage for you and me. When fish feel less pressured from predators, they often become very comfortable in that environment and are more likely to take a fly. The challenge is in these situations is seeing the fish.

A choppy surface distorts the image of anything below—making it incredibly difficult to sight fish. To overcome this obstacle, find a window in the turbulent water, any kind of smooth break. The clearing might be momentary. Strain your eyes to find it. When you fix on a slick-water window, lock on and follow it with your eyes. This allows you to scan through the window while it travels downstream, helping you effectively cover the water in front. When it works, it's a neat trick.

RIVER BOTTOM

If you are unable to find a viewing window, try looking for a shadow or some kind of movement below the surface. Despite the turbulence, you might still be able to see the shadow of a fish, even if it is somewhat distorted. This can be very helpful in bad light conditions and turbulent water where the waters source distorts the images below.

THE BUDDY SYSTEM

Sometimes two sets of eyes are better than one. I know I have been in many situations where there is good visibility on one side of the river and not the other. And of course by chance the side you need to cast from often has the worst viewing lanes. This is when the skill of your fishing partner comes in handy.

Have him direct you where to cast, and rely on him for when to set the hook or try a different presentation. Once you start employing this tag-team method with your fishing partner, you both will become comfortable giving each another directions that make sense. You will immediately "get" what your partner is telegraphing you.

Just makes sure whoever is sighting the trout from a high perch or opposite side of the river stays low so as to not spook the prize fish you're after.

Working as a team adds to the feeling of accomplishment when you both know you played a part in landing the trout of your lives.

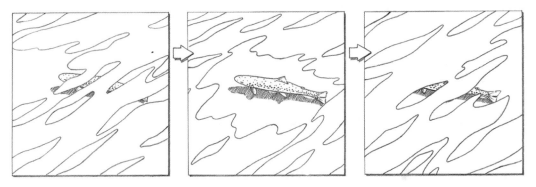

Learning to see hidden fish is essential. The hardest area in which to sight trout is rough, turbulent water. Such areas do not allow a lot of viewing opportunities. I discovered that there a section of slick water that moves downstream within the rough water—these slicks are your clear window to see down to the river bottom. Start at the top of the run or pool where you think the trout are holding. Then find a slick window and stare into it with unfocused eyes. Follow it downstream until you are able to cover the whole run. This will help you find large trout in water you thought was impossible to see into.

Look at the jaw on this pig that Angus Drummond is holding up. What a memorable afternoon catch.

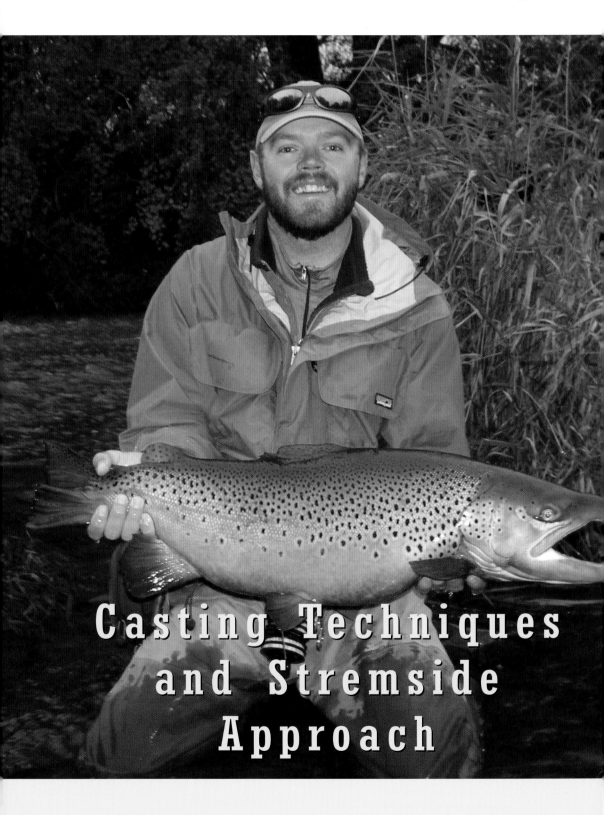

CHAPTER 5

Casting Techniques and Stremside Approach

ONE OF THE THINGS I ENJOY MOST about fishing for trophy trout is the thrill of the hunt. I love the suspense of wondering what's around the next bend and how big that fish might be. Even after you've fooled the giant into taking your fly, you still have the battle with him as he fights for his life before you savor the moment when he slides into your net.

And then there's the shared victory—your sense of accomplishment and the satisfying sight of the fish swimming away to fight another day. It doesn't get any better.

Pursuing large trout is both exciting and challenging. From the moment you sight your fish, you are facing multiple streamside obstacles and river situations still to overcome. Because you must face these challenges while simultaneously casting to a fish, being prepared to deal with and adjust to each situation can determine your success.

CHOOSING THE CAST

Having the ability to choose from several different casts when presented with a streamside challenge allows you the best opportunity to make a quality cast, resulting in an excellent drift and—with a little luck—a successful hook-up. The purpose of this chapter is to review casting fundamentals and discuss practical casts that I use routinely in a variety of real fishing situations. My four trusted casts in my tactical arsenal for trophy trout include:

- Conventional cast
- Steeple cast
- Roll cast
- Tension cast

THE CONVENTIONAL CAST

The conventional cast is a traditional casting stroke consisting of a stop at the 2 o'clock position on the back cast and a stop at the 10 o'clock position on the front cast.

The cast can be performed when there are no obstructions on the river. The conventional cast is often used because it the best way to achieve accuracy, maximum power and distance with each cast. Because no adjustments to the cast are necessary, you can perform a normal casting stroke within the 10 and 2 o'clock position. I've found that for the majority of people, this casting stroke is the most comfortable to perform.

While you can achieve accuracy, power, and distance with this cast, because the line is elevated above the water during the front and back part of the cast you must also contend with the increased risk of fish detecting and being spooked. If you use this cast, be sure to position yourself low and in a place on the water where the fish is less likely to see you and the line (preferably parallel with, or just behind the fish). The cast consists of five steps:

The first portion of this cast is the pickup. The pickup loads the energy in your rod, allowing you to start the false-casting sequence. With your line in the water in front of you, slightly elevate your rod and then proceed back with smooth acceleration and an abrupt stop at the 2 o'clock position.

Pause at the 2 o'clock position, allowing your line to straighten out behind you. This pause places a bend in your fly rod

Conventional Cast~There are situations when you need distance and speed to get your flies to the trout. A conventional cast is the most effective for accuracy with a long line. Deliver your offerings by simply stopping the rod at the 10 o'clock position. When you do everything right and execute well, your fly line shoots smoothly through the guides for a powerful and accurate presentation.

from the weight of your fly line, and also gives you the energy and power to perform the second step in the casting sequence, the forward casting stroke.

From the 2 o'clock position, smoothly accelerate your rod forward, making another abrupt stop at 10 o'clock.

Pause at the 10 o'clock position, and then start the back cast again. While performing this cast, it is imperative that you keep the rod traveling on a straight plane. This uniformity allows your line to perform tights loops and utilizes the maximum amount of energy from your fly rod. Continue this false-casting sequence until you reach the desired distance and accuracy.

When you are ready to present the fly to the fish, simply stop the rod on the forward cast at the 10 o'clock position, allowing your line to unroll, landing accurately and naturally on the water.

THE STEEPLE CAST

The steeple cast is most effective when a tall structure or objects behind you on the river prevent a normal back cast. This stroke allows you to perform a back cast that properly loads your rod and shoots the line forward 20 to 30 feet with minimal effort.

Start with the rod at the normal casting position, and then lift upward to the 2 o'clock position, making an abrupt stop at the 12 o'clock position. This back cast is designed to stop high, allowing the fly line to straighten out behind you without getting caught up in the obstacle and preventing you from executing a traditional cast.

Pause briefly at the 12 o'clock position and then accelerate forward smoothly, stopping abruptly at 10 o'clock in front.

Follow through with your rod to the surface of the water to finish the cast—the line shoots out of the rod in an accurate and straight form. Once the line lands, make the appropriate mend (if needed) and watch fly naturally drift toward the fish.

I have used this casting technique in countless encounters with large trout. Streamside vegetation or high banks along many rivers in many situations around the world often make a normal back cast impossible. In addition to these natural barriers to the back cast, there are also bodily limitations. I am commonly stuck in a small cove in a crouched position, afraid to move for fear of spooking a trout lying right in front of me. These tight spots on the water get even smaller when you're creeping into position to cast to a giant.

It's no coincidence that these tight

Steeple Cast~Cluttered streamsides prevent a conventional back cast. This is accentuated when hunting large trout because you are normally in a low-profile stance on the river's edge with structure behind you. A steeple cast is the way to make an accurate cast to the trout in tight quarters. Remember that the key to getting the best presentation is pausing long enough on the back cast when your rod is stopped at the 12 o'clock position, loading the rod properly with a shortened casting stroke.

spots often hold the largest trout. The big ones are counting on the protection such tight quarters afford. The steeple cast is the solution for getting your fly to these tucked-away fish. The trick is to deliver the cast without causing a disruptive splash. Even a relatively minor disturbance can be enough to spook the fish that could be the catch of a lifetime.

Practice the cast in non-fishing situations when there is no pressure or stress to do it right the first time. Find a large expanse of grass in a park or a neighborhood pond to perfect your technique. During "down time," I like to practice the cast on the river, picking a rock or structure as my target. This preparation has definitely helped me stay on top of my game, and it gives me the confidence to make the right presentation when it really counts.

THE ROLL CAST

When I'm out on the river, I rely primarily on the basic roll cast. The steps of performing the roll cast are easy to understand and perform, and the cast is efficient and effective. This cast can be used successfully in a variety of situations presented when casting to trophy trout, partly because the line spends less time in the air and thus has less chance of spooking wary fish.

I always point out to my clients the fact that this cast is not named for a rolling motion of the arm. The name is derived from the motion of the line rolling over itself in the air when it lifts off of the water's surface. The rolling of the line is vitally important when casting to the trout of a lifetime. If you make the mistake of rolling your arm, the rod tip will drop down to the water's surface. This drop causes a disturb-

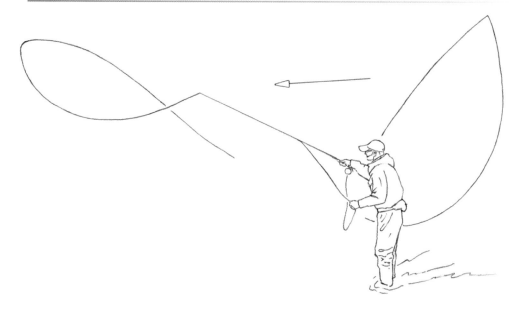

Roll Cast~Without question the roll cast is the most commonly used in trophy trout situations. It's effective in fishing both dry flies and nymph without a back cast. To perform properly, stop your rod tip at the 10 o'clock position in front of you. Your line lifts up off the water and rolls to the target in front of you without disturbing the water. I like to think of this cast as the forward motion of a conventional casting stroke.

ing splash resulting from your fly line rolling off the water (instead of the air) all the way to the trout. This bad habit is guaranteed to spook any sizeable fish you might have the chance of catching.

> ## AUTHOR'S TIP
>
> *Think of the roll cast as a forward motion of a normal casting stroke. This will stop your rod at the 10 o'clock position at the end of the cast, shooting your line up and forward and allowing it to lift and lay down gently, giving you a natural presentation of your fly.*

The low profile of this cast also allows you to be exceptionally accurate when presenting the fly. In addition to the steeple cast, this is another effective cast when there are obstacles behind you. There is no

back cast when performing this casting stroke. The rod loads with energy from the tension of the fly line on the water. The cast is broken down into three basic steps:

Start with your fly line in the water in front of you at a downstream angle. Gradually lift the rod from a horizontal position to a vertical 1 o'clock position, keeping the fly line in the water while performing the gradual lift.

Pause for a moment at the 1 o'clock position, and then tilt the rod tip at a slight angle away from your body. During this pause, you are creating tension on the fly line as it pulls in the water. This resistance loads your rod for the forward portion of your cast.

Begin the forward-casting stroke with smooth acceleration, making an abrupt stop high at the 10 o'clock position. This stop shoots the line up and forward, completing the cast. The secret is to stop high. This enables you to perform the cast correctly and get the most power and accuracy out of the cast.

The Tension Cast–One of the most productive ways for success on the water is a fast and accurate presentation. The tension cast gives you the opportunity for more casts to a trophy without spooking the fish—your line stays out of the air, keeping the trout from detecting frightening movement above.

Remember that the term "roll" in roll cast refers to the line rolling over itself—not to the rolling of your arm to perform the cast. It is hard to overcome the urge to drop your rod tip low on the forward part of this casting stroke. As the day grows long, the arm tends to get lazy from so many casts. But, if the rod stops at a low position, the line still shoots out in front of you and right in front of the target fish. Keep yourself disciplined by stopping the rod high at the 10 o'clock position when you come forward. When performed correctly, the fish will have no idea that you are anywhere in that area. Performing this cast correctly is like fishing in stealth mode—for this alone it's a great cast.

THE TENSION CAST

The tension cast is designed for speed and effectiveness. This cast allows you to cover water quickly and to make more presentations to a fish. The key to this cast is the placement of your rod tip when presenting the fly. The move consists of lifting the rod to a vertical position, pausing and then redirecting the rod upstream to make the cast.

The tension cast gives you an advantage due to fewer steps involved compared with other casts. Because there is no false casting involved, your line spends less time in the air, decreasing the chance of spooking the fish.

All right, this is one of the ugliest casts on the planet, but it gets the job done. I'm sure that many of my experienced clients see this cast and think, *How lazy do you have to be to cast like that?* It is true that there is no real skill involved when performing this flipping motion. But once my clients see this cast in action on the water, they adopt it immediately as their new go-to cast.

I always advise using the casting stroke that is most effective for the specific situation on the water—in other words, improvise. Not every cast is aesthetically pleasing. Some casting breaks the mold of the textbook stroke, but I'm not out there to look pretty! I am ready to catch huge trout employing any method that adds to my success.

Remember, the presentation of the tension cast allows you to get more casts to the fish quickly and with less effort. The measure of success is in the accuracy of your presentation. Because tension from the line in the water loads the rod, it is important to point your rod tip where you want the fly line and fly to go. Don't get lazy with your casting stroke and simply transfer your rod directly upstream from you. A sloppy transfer will cause your line to collapse, and you'll miss your target and the fish. The tension cast consists of two steps:

Starting with the fly line in the water downstream, lift your rod vertically to a 45-degree angle, pause for a second or two, and then find your target area.

Redirect the rod tip downward toward your target area in the water, stopping as the rod nears the horizontal position. This motion shoots your line to the target, presenting the fly properly.

I try to stay away from using the tension cast in shallow water because the fly lands on the surface and tends to make a mini explosion. But, when it comes to deeper water and to moving through runs quickly in the hopes of finding trophy fish, this cast is an ace in the hole.

Along with every aspect of the sport of fly fishing, casting has excited my passion. For the last five years, I have had the privilege of teaching anglers the basic and detailed techniques of the casting stroke in private lessons. Through this experience, I have found that many seasoned anglers who have been fly fishing leisurely throughout the years have developed bad habits in their casting that hinders both their distance and their accuracy. Like any sport that involves proper form, trying to "unlearn" these habits can be difficult; the challenge can feel overwhelming. Do yourself a favor: Give yourself a refresher from time to time. Going back to the basics will help you get all you can out of each cast and your precious time on the water.

THE APPROACH

Once you have spotted that trophy trout, your next challenge is getting into position to cast. Simple, right? Not so fast.

When approaching the fish, the most critical tactic of positioning is keeping a low profile. The excitement of seeing a trout of five pounds or greater finning serenely in clear, shallow water is enough to rattle any angler's nerves. The sight makes it difficult to keep one's cool.

Stop.

Take a deep breath.

Look around.

Force yourself to calmly and patiently observe the area to find the best position for casting to the fish. The fish isn't going anywhere. By keeping a low profile you reduce the chance that the trout may detect you and spook. If you rush the situation and spook the fish, you forfeit the opportunity to cast to a wide-open fish ripe for the picking.

Those who know me and have fished with me know that when I pursue trophy trout, my mantra is always, "Get down! Get down!" Whenever I see a trophy fish, I repeat this to myself, automatically stopping in my tracks while dropping down to one knee. I do this because it makes me think about the situation at hand and reduces the chances of my spooking the trout. This pause also gives me the chance to catch my breath, think, and simply relish the glorious moment at hand. Even as I write, I am reminiscing about all the monsters of the past that I contemplated while genuflecting.

AUTHOR'S TIP

Wear clothing that is dull in color and matches your surroundings. You want to be somewhat camouflaged when you're on the water. Remember that bright, bold colors—while they might look good on magazine covers—give the trout a better chance of detecting you.

When large trout are spooked, they can take up to five minutes to settle down and

I always take the time to admire a trophy catch, holding the precious fish as if there will never be another.

return to a feeding lane. Some never return. By staying low and keeping yourself out of the trout's line of sight, you will get the chance to cast to a happy, stress-free fish—a fish that is 100 times more likely to mistake your fly for something good to eat. Crawl if you have to. Better that you eat dirt. Once the trout is gone, it's gone. You'll always have soap and water.

While doing your best to keep a low profile, it's also important to maintain constant sight of the fish. This gives you the advantage of being able to adjust should the fish move while you are crawling into position. Keeping a keen eye on the fish gives you the added benefit of observing its rhythm of movement, which is particularly valuable if the fish is feeding. Use this knowledge to time your drift.

If you do everything right, you'll be rewarded by watching that fabulous moment when the fish takes your fly.

THE ABC TECHNIQUE

As a fly fishing guide, I have the advantage of learning at a faster rate than if I were fishing on the river by myself—even if I could fish practically every day of the year. When I am guiding anglers, I'm not just focusing on the fish and the best technique for catching them. In addition to the fish and the technique, a guide must also observe everything surrounding, including the client. With each trip, I learn something new.

One trip stands out. I had been fishing since I was a kid, but this was only my third trip as a professional guide. My client was a 72-year-old man who was a true sportsman. He and I fished with some success for four hours in the morning, and with the chit chat between casting strokes, we began building a rapport and learning about each other's lives. While we took a break for lunch and refueled for the afternoon fish-

ing, he popped the question that would change my way of approaching trout for the rest of my life.

"Son," he asked. "Do you know your ABCs?"

I was speechless. I looked at him with a weak smile that belied my mystification and maybe minor terror *There is no way that he means what I think he does*, I thought.

Thank goodness, he didn't. He proceeded to tell me about a method of approaching wary trout that I am about to pass onto you in revised form.

"I think anglers generally try to make this sport too hard," he said. "They over-think everything at hand. Sometimes knowing the small things makes the big difference."

Words of wisdom coming from a wise and deep-rooted angler—what more is there to say?

That afternoon, my client took the time to generously guide *me*, showing me the right way to get into position to make a cast. Now I feel fortunate sharing with you such a simple concept that yields such exceptional results.

I had been guilty of rushing things when I saw a big fish. I was like a bucking bronco, hot and eager to get my fly in the fish's face. My impatience was controlling my moves. Yet I was smart enough to realize my shortcomings weren't helping my cause. To counter the errant effects of enthusiasm in my own fishing led me to adopt this system for effectively approaching a trophy fish in those heart-thumping situations.

When you first spot a trophy fish, it is imperative that you stop and immediately observe your surroundings. Plan your strategy of moving into position for casting. At the same time, scan the water. Get an idea of what to expect should the fish run and demand that you follow it upstream or down.

The ABC technique consists of choosing three possible areas to approach the fish and get you into position when it is time to cast. Mentally mark each spot with a letter: A, B, and C. This delineation forces you to consider more than one casting position while also affording you the time to think over the situation at hand. By thinking about possible casting positions, you will prepare yourself to make a more logical (and often more effective) decision. This mental marking may also help you find an area that wasn't your first choice but could present itself as the most successful choice.

Ideally, your casting position should be in an area that keeps you as undetectable as possible, allows you to maintain a constant view of the fish, and insures a proper presentation. Once you have determined your position, stay low and cautious. By knowing the surroundings and taking time to find your spot, you will learn more from each experience and become more effective when casting to trophy fish.

I am forever thankful to the old angler for freely opening his treasure chest of knowledge from what, I am sure, was a lifetime of many awesome fishing adventures. I am also indebted to him for revealing to me the beauty of generously sharing angler "secrets." This spirit of comradery is what enhances our sport and causes it to become more special with each new season.

Try these methods the next time you are on the water and discover the visual advantage you gain over the trout. Happy hunting!

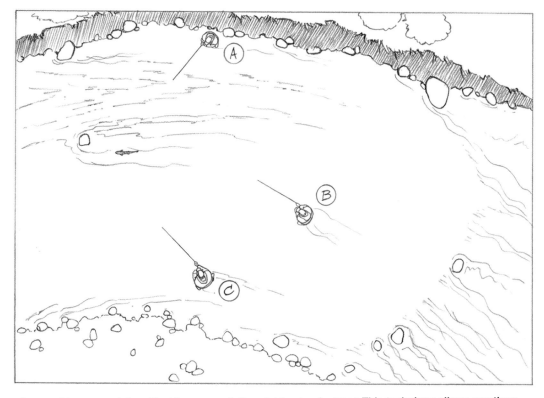

Streamside approach is critical to successfully catching trophy trout. This technique allows you three possible areas to cast from when you make a presentation—A, B and C. Having more than one area to choose from forces you to determine where you should stand in delivering the most natural drift of your fly. This greatly improves your chances of getting multiple cast to your target trout without spooking it.

CHAPTER 6

The Dotted-Line Technique

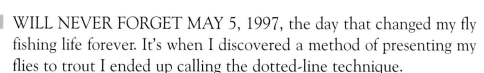

I WILL NEVER FORGET MAY 5, 1997, the day that changed my fly fishing life forever. It's when I discovered a method of presenting my flies to trout I ended up calling the dotted-line technique.

It was a normal outing on my favorite section of dream stream, the South Platte River—five and a half miles of trout-fishing paradise, where every cast brings the opportunity of catching a fish that I knew could make my dreams come true.

The day started out like any other. I was fishing water where I had success before, occasionally hooking up here and there. I continued fishing the run for a while, and then I decided it was time to move. I started walking upstream, scanning the water for trout. I had a good feeling about this day— I just knew something great was going to happen. And boy was I right.

I soon stumbled upon a shallow section of even-moving water dropping into a long, riffled run. *This looks like good water,* I thought to myself. I was confident there had to be something big here. Then I saw it: a large red gill plate of a huge rainbow trout. It looked like a bright submerged apple in the river. I couldn't believe any trout could be so massive. I quickly pulled out a bunch of line out and shot a cast above the fish. The cast was just past the trout—I thought I had blown it. Just then the jaws of this beauty opened wide as it took my fly. The violent head shakes on the surface of the water were unbelievable.

Then it hit me like a ton of bricks. "I wasn't off when I cast past the trout; the flies naturally drift back to me not straight down. That means the flies were in this giants feeding lane." I thought to myself. I was so excited with my new discovery and the trophy I had on, I could hardly keep my composure. So I did what any enthusiastic angler would do, I shouted out "Yes" at the top of my lungs!

This was my introduction to the "dotted-line" technique—the name I've given to an exceptionally effective method for convincing a trophy trout to take your fly. After landing the 7-pound male rainbow, I thought through the steps leading to its capture. The conclusion I reached was simple: In this situation the technique was what had mattered most. That's why the giant had taken my fly.

You can put my experience to work on the river next time you are presented with an opportunity to hook a trophy. You too will immediately become a believer.

UNDERSTANDING THE DOTTED LINE

The dotted-line technique is used to properly present the fly in the fish's feeding lane by laying the foundation for a natural presentation, proper hook set, and—ultimately—a successful hook-up. Fundamentally, the dotted-line technique consists of (1) locating the trout, (2) determining its depth in the water, (3) visualizing the target area to cast to, and (4) making the cast. If you cast correctly and your fly lands in the target area, it will be perfectly aligned to drift right into the fish's mouth.

In conventional methods of fly fishing, common practice is to read water to determine where the fish is and then cast in the

John Wexler admiring a nice eight-pound brown before sending it kicking off to fight another day.

general area. After you cast, the next step is normally to throw a mend in your line, hoping your fly proceeds downstream in a drag-free drift. While this method sometimes works when your target is a body of water, it is not as effective when sight-fishing to a specific trophy trout. I soon realized that there had to be a better way to make a natural presentation to a trophy I could see—while being as accurate as possible. This challenge is what encouraged me to create the dotted-line technique. In my experience it's the single most effective way to sight-fish to any giant in every discipline of fly fishing.

Ask yourself this question: how many times have you seen a trout holding in the water and while your presenting your flies to this beast, you have no idea if the trout can see your flies? If this sounds familiar, don't worry these techniques are the cure.

In this chapter we'll discuss in detail the steps and strategies of this technique, so that you can start trying this extremely effective method the next time you're on the river.

One of the nice things about the dotted-line technique is its versatility. It can be used in all kinds of fishing scenarios (fishing underwater with nymphs, fishing to risers with dries, stripping streamers, etc.). It is also useful with a variety of fishing rigs (nymphing, with or without a strike indicator, one or more flies, etc). For this initial discussion and for ease of explanation, the rig in the following scenario consists of one or two flies, split-shot weight, and a pinch-on strike indicator.

Step 1 – Creating the Dotted Line

Once you get a visual on the trout holding in the water, start watching. Really watch—observe intently the flow of water in front of the fish, any surrounding objects in the water, and how the water moves as it approaches the trout's holding spot. Now, in your mind, draw an imaginary dotted line from the trout's head to an area two or three feet upstream of the trout. This is the target at which you will cast your fly, allowing it to flow through the trout's feeding zone.

Step 2 – Determining the "Cast To" Area

The distance from the trout to the target spot where you cast is determined by the depth of water the trout is holding in. For example, in shallow water the distance between the trout and the spot you cast to is shorter because it takes less time for the fly to sink to the depth at which the fish is holding; whereas, in deeper water, the distance upstream from the fish you drop your fly should be increased because it takes the fly longer to sink to the depth of the trout.

The approximate distance of the imaginary dotted line in shallow water is about two to three feet. In deeper water, this distance increases to four to five feet—even more, depending on the depth.

In my years of guiding, one of the most valuable things I have learned is to pay close attention to what my flies are doing below the surface of the water. It's essential for a good angler to know how to adjust if conditions require the fly to sink slower or faster. If you are fishing a shallow body of water and you have the sense something is off with your drift—or you continually snag the bottom—do not hesitate to adjust the amount of weight you have on. Also consider changing the distance from your indicator to split shot.

I always try to have fun on the river by challenging myself with every big trout I encounter. It's a guessing game between me and the fish. Adapting in difficult situations not only helps your success rate on the river but also increases your knowledge and helps you become the most effective angler you can possibly be.

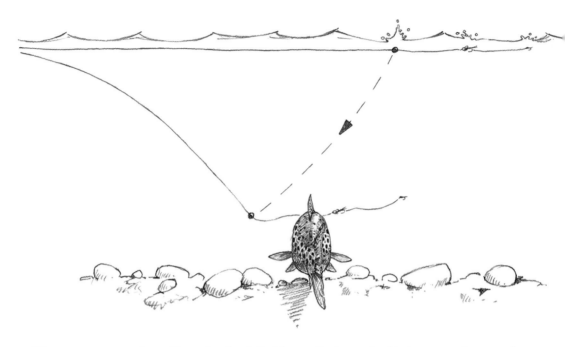

Whenever you present your flies using the dotted-line method, you should always cast just past the trout. The reason is that your flies sink by gradations while drifting toward you—they never sink straight down. With that in mind, if you place the flies directly above the trout and not past it, they would sink toward you and move out of the fish's feeding lane. By compensating for the direction in which your flies drift you will allow more trophies a chance to see and take your rig.

AUTHOR'S TIP

Your target area, as shown in Figure X, should be just beyond the imaginary dotted line. When your fly sinks in the water, if it doesn't sink straight down in a vertical fashion, the fly gradually travels back toward you as it sinks. If you were to land the fly directly on the imaginary line, the fly starts to drift back naturally toward you, missing the trout's feeding zone— literally coming up shot, which is something you don't want.

Step 3 – Practice the Cast (Line Adjustment)

After you have determined the dotted line and the target area to cast to, pull out enough line to reach the trout and make a couple of practice casts downstream from the fish. This gives you the opportunity to determine precisely how far you need to cast and keeps your line and fly out of the trout's viewing window, reducing the risk of spooking the fish. You want the length of line to be long enough to be able to cast just past the imaginary dotted line, without being too long as this will result in the line rubbing the fish. Line control is critical. Take care to use *only the amount of line* needed to make the cast and complete the drift. You don't want too much slack, which impedes the hook set and may also spook the fish.

If you still question the length of line—

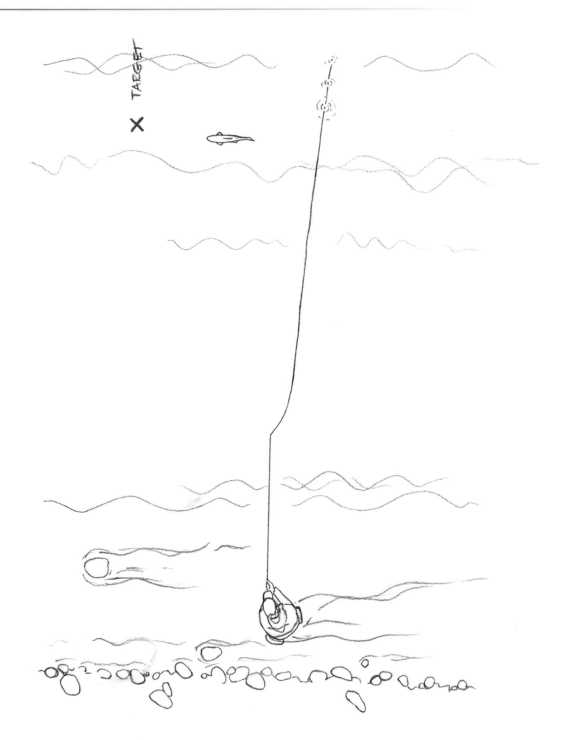

When you are determining how much line required to perform the dotted-line presentation, you should practice a cast or two downstream from the trout. This will keep the fish from detecting movement or light reflecting off your fly line and spooking. If you are not sure if the length of line you have out is correct, think short and let the fly drift past short of the trout. You will then have a better idea of how much line you need to make a perfect cast. This practice approach has rewarded me with numerous spot-on casts to large trout that otherwise would have spooked. And a spooked trout won't eat your fly.

John Barr fooled this huge male with his go-to red Copper John.

or if the distance is correct—cast short of the fish and adjust accordingly. This way, if your fly is not in the correct position, you can allow the fly to drift downstream of the fish, and recast. This decreases the chance of your spooking the fish and allows you another chance to cast to your target. Using this technique of determining the length of line downstream from the fish, my fishing companions and I have practically without fail been able to get within five to 10 feet of that fish of a lifetime.

I am here to tell you that your heart at this moment is pumping so loud and hard, you can't hear anything else. I guess this is what they call being "in the zone." The only reason we're able to get so close is because the fish has no chance of detecting you in his viewing lane. This is awesome, because you are able to see the detailed image of the trout and its behavior.

Step 4 — Presenting the Fly

After you make a few practice casts behind the fish to get the proper distance with a comfortable cast, you are now ready to make your presentation. When you present the fly to the area above the trout, imagine the dotted line where you want your fly and weight to slash down. You want your fly line, leader, and tippet vertically in front of one another when the cast is made.

The most difficult part for many anglers is controlling the cast. Most are used to stopping their rod high on their forward cast, allowing their fly to kick over and land on the water. This is very effective when fishing dries but it can cause a problem when throwing heavier nymphs or streamers.

What happens is the weight on your rig causes your flies to turn over aggressively. Each time they hit the water they land in a different spot. This is a huge problem considering you may have only a shot or two at

the big fish in front of you. Lack of precision permits the trout to see your leader or weights before the flies, because you flies landed up stream of your fly line instead of perpendicular or straight across.

To fix this problem, use a pick-up-and-lay-down cast. Let your rod tip stop just above the water's surface on your forward cast and presentation. I often allude to hammering nails. This gives you pinpoint accuracy in presenting your flies. After applying a mend in your line, the first thing to drift into the giant trout's feeding lane is your imitation.

AUTHOR'S TIP

When determining the length of line, keep in mind your rig set-up. For example, if are fishing with one fly with a micro-shot weight approximately 12 inches above the fly and the strike indicator four feet from your weight, when you are executing your "practice" cast, your strike indicator should be approximately four or five feet from the fish. And you should see your weights splash on, or near, the imaginary dotted line.

The reason for this straight layout of your rig is so, when you apply a mend, it moves your fly line and leader upstream. This gives you a natural drift. It also assures that the first thing visible to the fish is your fly. If your fly line, leader, and tippet do not land vertically—in the desired straight line—the fish will see your weight or leader or both. If it's the first thing visible in its feeding lane, it will spook. By keeping your presentation straight and applying a mend,

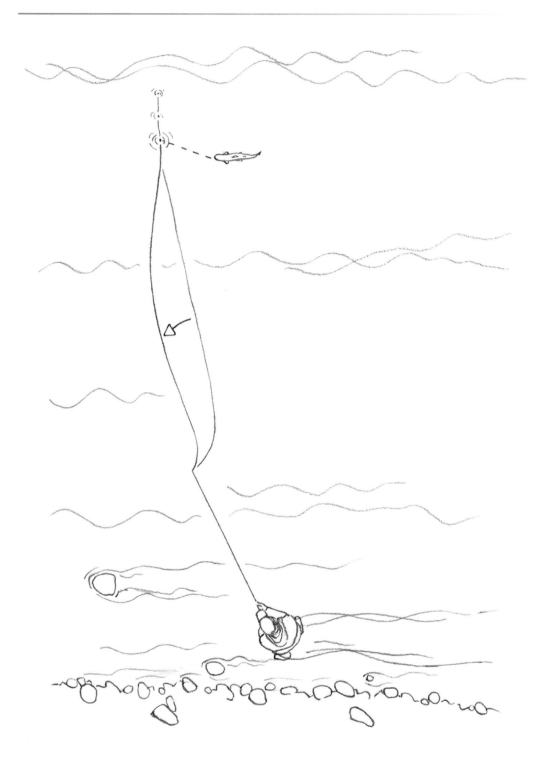

To execute the dotted-line technique effectively, your flies must be the fist thing visible to the trout in its viewing lane. Apply a mend in your fly line and leader after your flies have landed on the imaginary dotted line. This will move your rig upstream and keep the flies drifting in front of the leader, thus preventing the trout from detecting anything unnatural, greatly increasing the chance of it taking one of them.

the first thing the fish sees is your fly.

Being comfortable in knowing you can throw a good presentation to the fish is not easy at first but don't get frustrated. Practice, practice, *practice*. Eventually it becomes second nature; you will be on point every time. After presenting your fly and throwing a mend, you should then focus your attention on the fish and the fly line, including the strike indicator if you are using one. (However, do not focus too much attention on the indicator—avoid the common mistake of watching the strike indicator and not the fish!)

Watch the fish for any subtle or aggres-

AUTHOR'S TIP

If the fly passes downstream and the fish does not strike, allow the fly to drift at least a couple of feet past the fish before you recast. This prevents foul-hooking the fish or rubbing your leader against the trout, thereby spooking it. It also allows you to make multiple casts quickly.

Using 2X tippet helped Sean Mayer adjust to this trout's furious head shakes right after the hook-up.

A prime pre-spawn 'bow: fat, fresh and full of fury. I love early spring action on small water.

sive movements when it takes your fly. It's okay to periodically look to see where your line is to determine where your fly is and figure out if you need to make a mend to maintain a natural drift.

When the fish commits and takes your fly, the first step in catching a trophy has been accomplished.

USING THE DOTTED-LINE IN SHALLOW WATER

Shallow-water situations are a personal favorite of mine. Man, are they exciting. Not just because you see the fish and all its movements but the explosion that occurs afterward when the fish tries to get away can freak you out to the point where your whole body goes numb—what a thrill! I'm serious when I say this, it can down right scare anglers with the explosion after the fish takes the fly in shallow water.

I will never forget the lady fly fisher I took out recently. She was quite a character.

Most anglers enjoy the serenity and peaceful escape of fly fishing. Immersing oneself in a natural, quiet environment is wonderfully relaxing. Well, not if you were on the water near my client the other day. This no joke: Every time we hooked a trout, she belted out a horrible sounding scream at the top of her lungs. My first response when this was, "What the heck?" I wish I had a large hood to put over my head at that moment. Every other angler on the water had his eyes glued on us. This continued for the next few hook-ups.

Okay, this is getting out of control, I thought. But I soon realized after four or five ear-ringing screams that she couldn't anticipate the strike of these powerful trout in shallow water. Each explosive grab caught her off guard.

I must admit that a first hook-up in the shallows is a very intense moment. So I decided that it was what it was—and joined in the festivities. I thought, *Why not make the most of the trip?* Next time you hear a scream that sounds as if someone is wrestling a shark in a creek, don't worry. It's my angler and she's having a blast.

The dotted-line technique can be executed in various fishing situations including shallow water where the fish is exposed. Here it is easiest for the angler to determine when the fish eats and also how deep the fish is. However, the trick to shallow water is to not use too much weight. This causes you to snag the bottom or make your fly drift unnaturally, spooking the fish or deterring it from eating your fly. Always start light when applying weight and then adjust by adding more if you are not deep enough. This saves you from an improper drift.

The cast in a shallow body of water is normally shorter in length when presented in front of the fish, because the sinking rate is short. In the shallowest of water, mending is not needed because when you mend, slack is taken out of your line, increasing the sinking speed of your fly. By applying too many mends in shallow water you decrease the length of your drift after the presentation because the water is not deep.

Fast, shallow water is the best situation to catch trophy trout. The window in which the trout sees its food is lessened due to the fact that the distance from its eyes to the surface of the water is shorter. The fish reacts quickly because it has less time to investigate its food. More times than not, due to their opportunistic and aggressive behavior they commit and take the fly.

USING THE DOTTED-LINE IN DEEPER WATER

Deeper water is often more challenging for presenting the fly to the fish. Increased factors come into play. Because the distance from the trout's eyes to the surface of the water is increased, the feeding lane becomes wider and more abundant. The trout then has more time to see and investigate the fly. With this in mind, achieving a near-natural, drag-free drift is crucial in having success—the fly appears real. The likelihood of the trout's eating your fly increases. This means you should apply numerous mends throughout your drift to get your fly deep and maintain a drag-free presentation. This makes your fly seem like a genuine insect floating in the river.

Another key factor in fishing deep water is to find the area in the river where the fish is holding. Approximately how many feet below the surface is the fish? To determine this you have to rule out depth by trial and error, and apply weight gradually. Remember to start light. If the fish doesn't strike—or you can see the fly float above the fish, out of its feeding zone—apply more weight until you reach the level of water in which the fish is feeding.

In such a situation, understanding what your fly is doing below the surface of the water is vital. Don't be reluctant to add more weight and go very deep. Trout do not always hold in the same water column, and a good number of times the largest trout tend to hug the bottom. This secret can help you reach the fish quickly.

When you are presenting a fly to a fish in deeper water, the distance from where your fly lands in the water to where the fish is holding increases markedly. This allows your fly time to sink; it allows you time to mend and achieve a natural drift. When fishing a streamer or baitfish imitation, you are simulating trout food that moves. You should apply the same principles, adding distance between the fly and the fish, and casting farther past the fish. This allows your streamer to sink to the depth of the fish. The longer cast past the fish allowing you to start stripping the fly before it hits the fish's feeding zone. This helps makes the fly appear more like a moving baitfish or forage-food source.

Let me tell you, some of the most unbelievable visual strikes I have encountered are while fishing streamers in clear water. Sometimes I feel I'm going mad. Every time I retrieve the fly and a fish follows, it's like I have a nervous twitch. When I think the giant is going to strike, I react almost having set. Talk about rattled nerves! But once the fish does hit, its lights out and I am ready and on point.

The dotted-line technique inevitably becomes less precise when the zone expands between the fly and the fish, but you have the advantage of easier adjustment—the fly is in motion and you can increase the length of your strips to bring the fly in closer if you have cast too far. Once the fly is in the feeding zone, a fish frequently follows the fly before striking it. This results in many strikes coming at a 45-degree angle downstream toward the end of the presentation. The first half of the drift is more for preparation until you reach the fish's feeding zone.

AUTHOR'S TIP

Always remember when you are casting to a fish using the dotted-line technique is to always think short. This means that if you cast short of the feeding zone, you can readjust and cast farther without spooking the fish because it won't see the rig or fly. But if you cast too far past the fish, you may spook it and lose the chance to ever hook it.

The best indicator is watching the fish when using the dotted- line technique. It is the most effective way to present the fly to a fish you can see while maintaining the greatest accuracy. In my experience, the technique is universally the very best way to catch superior trout on a fly. It has never failed me. I'll never again fish using other methods. The dotted-line technique is simply the way to go.

I am blown away by young Logan Clark's ability to catch trout—I can't wait to see what he lands in the future.

Fighting an Oversized Trout

THE TOUGHEST CHALLENGE in freshwater fly fishing is fighting and landing a huge trout on a small fly and a light tippet. Because the weight of the fish usually exceeds the breaking strength of the tippet material, the secret is to use fish-fighting strategies that allow you to bring the fish to the net without applying so much pressure that the line breaks—or too little pressure, allowing the fish to work the hook free.

I always listen to that voice in my head that says, *If you think you are applying to much pressure, you probably are.* Trust your instincts when you're fighting that trophy. I understand it's hard to stay calm and focused when the thrill of hooking the largest trout you've ever seen sends adrenaline coursing through your body but, by trusting your instincts and knowledge, you will be triumphant. It's raw excitement!

Large fish are most often lost right at the very beginning or the end of the fight—during the first 10 seconds or so after being hooked, or as they are brought in close to the net. When a large trout is first hooked, it usually makes a series of strong head-shakes followed by a long run. Being prepared to react is the key to success. In this chapter I will discuss:
- Setting the hook
- What to expect after the set is made
- Rod positioning and adjustments
- "Walking the dog"—a surefire technique for fighting fish
- Guiding trout around structure

SETTING THE HOOK

Setting the hook is the first step in successfully fighting a super-sized trout. Doing it right is critical. The end result of landing or losing the fish is determined by how effectively you set the hook at the start. When a trout eats, the instinctive reaction by many anglers is to set the hook in a straight-up motion. No problem using this standard technique on average-sized trout, but when the stakes are higher, you risk los-

ing a potential trophy.

There's a more effective way. It's all about timing and power. Timing is waiting until you know the trout has taken your fly before setting and giving the fish sufficient time to open and close its over-sized jaws on the fly. Smaller trout are quick. They grab their food and are gone in a flash. It takes a large fish more time to open their jaws and consume the food. If you set the hook too soon, you'll pull the fly out of the fish's mouth without even penetrating its jaw.

If you can see the fish clearly, watch the fish instead of the strike indicator or fly. When you see the fish take the fly or turn its head, make the set. To effectively set the hook, you need to apply a smooth acceleration of power at exactly the right time. This is accomplished by lifting the rod downstream and with an upward angle until you feel an ample amount of tension on your rod. When you reach this point, keep your rod in the same position to maintain sufficient pressure on the fish.

Along with timing, the application of power is another important element in setting the hook on a big fish. By applying too

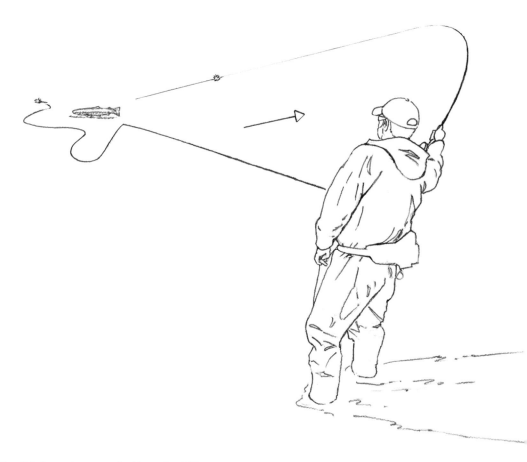

The fish has taken your fly. Now what? The proper way to set the hook on a big trout is by lifting your rod—not by applying a fast, aggressive motion which can cause the tippet material to break from the shock of power. If you lift the rod at a downstream angle, you will place the fly in the corner of the trout's mouth, not on the top of the jaw lined with sharp teeth. This placement allows you to apply maximum power during the fight while maintaining control over the trout. Remember, when the trout eats the hook has already partially penetrated its mouth when it is pulled down by the current. You are simply assuring that the fly is stuck firmly in the giant's mouth when you lift and set the hook.

much power, you will reach the breaking strength of your leader or tippet, resulting in breaking off the fish. However, if you don't apply enough power on the set, you can lose the fish later in the fight when your fly dislodges from the fish's mouth. There is a fine line with how much pressure to apply.

"Practice makes perfect", as the old saying goes, and time will help you learn this skill. Make a smooth downstream set by lifting your rod rather than making a sudden jerk. Some anglers have a tendency to make a big set using a jerking action, bringing the rod past their head, which I refer to as the

"Bill Dance" hook set. These aren't bass and you don't want to rip their lips off. This may be effective in other fishing situations, but not when fly fishing for trout, especially large ones. I like to think of the hook set as a lift of the rod. If you think about it, you are simply reassuring your fly after it has started to penetrate the trout's jaw.

When practicing the hook set with clients—something I do religiously—I tell them to lift the rod in a downstream direction and upward, similar to the motion of preparing for the next cast. We practice this 10 to 15 times so they get the feel and

A trophy is not always the biggest fish you catch. The colors of this rainbow made it my catch of the day.

rhythm of "just lifting" at a downstream angle, versus trying to launch the fish onto the bank. After this short exercise, they are more comfortable and the hook set becomes more of an automatic motion. In my experience, going through this little drill as a practice session before an angler hooks his first "WOW" fish, significantly increases the success in setting the hook properly.

When you set the hook on a giant trout, brace yourself for violent headshakes, which happen almost instantly after the hook set. Unless you are fishing a heavy leader to throw streamers or baitfish imitations, use discretion. Many serious anglers I have been around are all guilty of setting too hard. Fortunately, it takes only one show-stopping moment watching a miniature spotted whale leaving town with your fly in its jaw and your limp leader flapping in the breeze and you'll never again forget to set the hook with finesse.

To ensure the proper placement of your fly, apply your set at a downstream angle. This will place the fly at the corner of the fish's jaw, around the maxillary bone. This keeps the fly and the tippet away from the hardest part of the jaw which is usually lined with small, sharp teeth. When setting the hook with a downstream motion, your rod should be at a 45-degree angle. This angle allows you to maintain constant tension on the fish.

When I fish for trophy trout, I am usually casting to, hooking, and fighting the fish while positioned slightly downstream of the trout. This is a huge advantage when trying to keep the hooked fish from breaking off. You want leader, tippet, and fly to stay away from the front part of the trout's jaw, which along with having a lot of teeth, is the hardest part of the trout's mouth. This can make it difficult to get full penetration when your fly is placed there, not to mention how fast one of those teeth can cut

through your tippet.

There is nothing more depressing than standing upstream of a giant trout watching him open his mouth, take your fly, thrash around on the surface, and then vanish as your line bounces back into your face, as if to say, "No, today is not the day, you're going to catch me!" Setting at a downstream angle will help keep your rig out of the danger zone of the trout's mouth and will likely save you from a heartbreaking experience.

AFTER YOU SET THE HOOK

When you first set the hook the fish normally starts violently shaking its head, beneath the surface or sometimes when leaping completely out of the water, followed by an aggressive run. And when I say violently, I mean violently.

The actions by the fish are so extreme that the trout's head is almost touching its tail with each bending movement. This is when your nerves kick in and the adrenaline starts to flow. Don't worry, this is normal. To this day, I still get so "jazzed" that my rod tip will start to wiggle side to side from me shaking or just feeling the affects of the adrenaline. Stay focused and continue the heart-pounding fight.

Most large trout are lost during these first frantic 30 seconds. Whenever you feel the thumping headshakes from a fish, it is doing its best to dislodge the fly. Feeling the amount of power applied on your rod when the fish is head shaking will surely get your heart pumping.

Now is the time to remember: *The tug is the drug!*

Allow your arm to act as an extension of your rod. Drop your arm slightly, keeping your elbow down, to cushion the pressure of each headshake and then return the rod to its original upright position. When the fish makes a dashing run and you feel intense

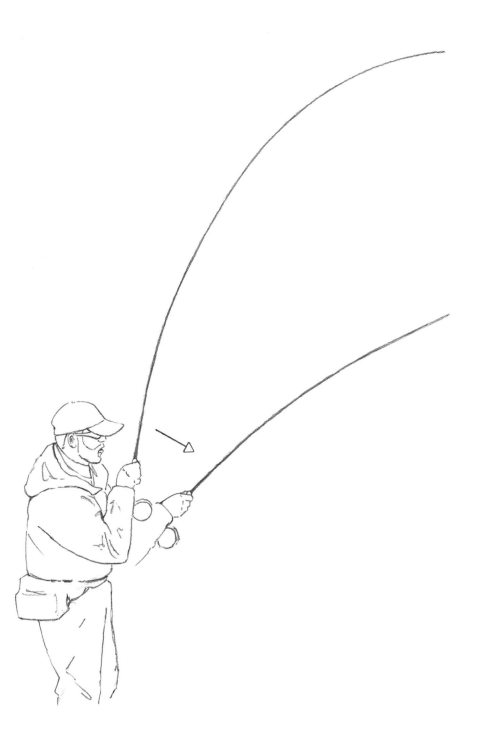

The first reaction from any giant trout is to shake its head. These violent thrusts are the primary reason most fish are lost in the first 15 seconds of each fight. I have hooked some trophies that have pulled my arm down almost three feet with each head shake. To compensate and keep the fish on, allow your arm to be pulled down slightly with each head-shaking thrust, then return it to a vertical fighting position. This absorbs some of the tension on your tippet material, preventing the trout from breaking off.

Matt Wilkerson putting maximum pressure on a hot trout at the inlet to Spinney Reservoir. Notice how Matt's rod is positioned in front of his body—this allows him to easily drop his arm when the fish runs.

pressure on your line, adjust by lowering your rod to a semi-horizontal position, allowing your reel to absorb the pressure of the run and the line to be freely stripped, and finally, return it to the downstream vertical position.

By learning to adjust to the feel of the tension and pressure applied by the fish, you will be much more successful in keeping the fish "hooked up" during this critical phase in the battle. Remember, slack line is your enemy. Also, be sure to keep a bend in your rod when you make the adjustments—this keeps constant pressure on the fish.

When the fish makes a strong run away from you, allow the trout to pull your arm to a nearly horizontal position. Although many anglers have been taught to *raise* the rod tip—and that you never point the rod at the fish—experience has taught me that the drag system of a quality reel is better than you are at maintaining even line tension during a strong run. Let the reel do its job. The flexing of the slightly raised rod tip acts as a cushion.

I wish I had a dollar for every time one of my clients touches the reel when the fish takes off across river. I'm sure other anglers on the water get tired of hearing me yelling, "Don't touch the reel, let it run!" It is a natural reaction for many, because the first fishing experience in most anglers' life is with conventional gear, which allows you to reel at the same time the drag is releasing line. So I'll shout it one more time to make sure you hear me, "Don't touch the reel—*let the fish run!*"

As soon as the fish slows or stops its run, move your rod to a more vertical position to take up the slack in the line. This allows the rod tip to act as a shock absorber to counteract any sharp tugs on the line during the fight. The dampening effect decreases the chances of breaking your tippet, but be ready to lower the rod if the fish runs again. This technique is remarkably helpful. It's kept me from losing fish in countless situations.

Wild trout, especially pressured trout, are constantly alert for anything that wants to kill and eat them; they know instinctively where to run to escape danger. Because a large trout's body structure and tail are so broad and muscular, a couple of thrusts from a hooked fish sends it bolting upstream or down in seconds. By allowing your rod tip to drop during this burst of energy, like a smart prizefighter, you'll maintain an advantage over the fish.

ROD POSITIONING AND ADJUSTMENTS

One simple advantage an angler has in fighting a large trout is the ability to make an adjustment with the placement of your

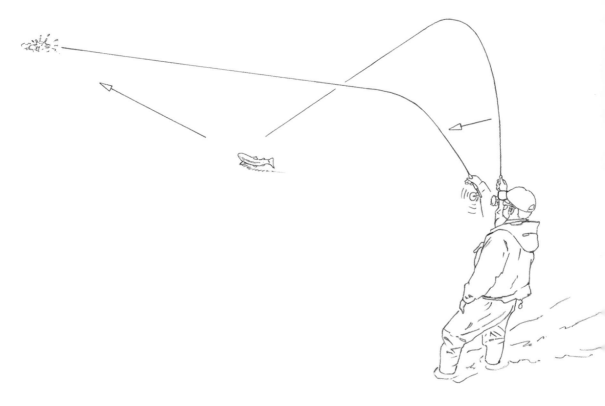

After a trophy is done head shaking it usually blasts off in a long powerful run, trying to escape and head for cover. If you keep your rod at a high vertical position during the run, the fish has a better chance of breaking off when the rod is fully flexed. To compensate for these powerful runs, you should drop your rod to a nearly horizontal position, allowing the smooth drag on your reel to apply the tension. This will help prevent the tippet from breaking, while applying enough tension to keep the monster on.

rod. This compensates for each powerful move the fish makes. The size, weight, and strength of the fish is enough to break your tippet, but being able to adjust when too much tension is applied will keep you from breaking off your trophy.

The best way to keep a consistent amount of tension on the fish is to slightly raise and lower your arm and the rod tip simultaneous with the headshakes, so the rod tip flexes with each shake. Lower the rod tip about a foot with each shake, and then return it to the original position immediately. The rod should appear to be an extension of your arm. This takes pressure off of the knots in the line, lessens the pressure on the fly so it doesn't dislodge, and continues to wear down the fish by forcing it to pull against the pressure of the rod and line.

AUTHOR'S TIP

By forcing the fish to continually pull against the pressure of the rod and line the trout will tire more quickly and give you the edge in fighting your trophy.

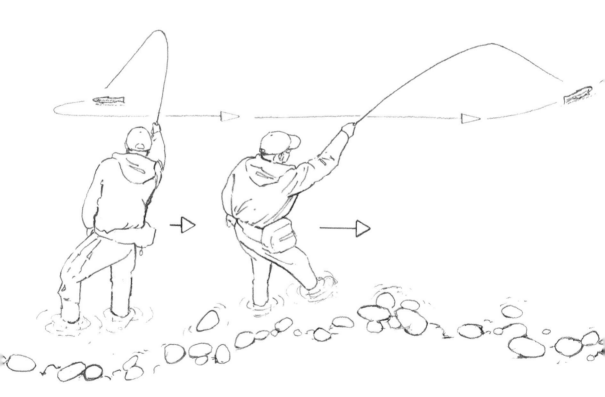

The best way you can tire out a trophy trout is to have the least amount of line out during the fight while applying the maximum amount of pressure. I like the phrase "walking the dog." When training a dog you keep it right next to you so you have control. The same concept applies when fighting a trout: If the fish goes upstream or down, follow it, remaining perpendicular to the fish with your rod in a vertical position. This causes the trout to tire out by fighting against the pressure it feels on the top of its jaw.

During almost all fights there are lulls in the action when the fish stops and holds steady in a certain spot, or swims toward you. When this happens, slowly and gradually lower your rod tip, quickly gain as much line as you can, then return your rod to the original position. Always maintain pressure on the fish as you retrieve line. This allows you to keep the distance of line from you to the fish as short as possible. So many anglers are afraid to keep a good amount of pressure on the trout when they gain line or are simply trying to lift the fish's head. Man, lay the wood to them! These state-of-the-art rods and reels are designed to handle the pressure.

"Reel, reel, *reel!*" is what I'm usually holler at my friends or clients when someone hooks a big fish, encouraging them to control slack line and take charge of the battle. Their wide-eyed blank reaction usually says it all. And at the end of the fight, however, they normally remark at how blown away they are at the ability to reel up so much line and get so close to the fish during the fight.

The distance between you and the fish is critical. The more line you have out, the more control the fish will have. Because you are not able to apply pressure above the fish, you forfeit the ability to control the situation—allowing the rampaging monster to do whatever it wants. Keeping the fish on a short leash and gaining line at every opportunity throughout the fight shortens the space between you and the fish. You keep maximum pressure on the trout and tire it out quickly, thus contributing to a high likelihood of safe revival when the tussle is over.

WALKING THE DOG

To fight big trout on light tippet, you must have a solid understanding of your equipment and its capabilities—not the technical specifications of your rod's construction, or how many pieces and parts make up your reel's drag system—but rather how all the various elements of your gear are used to overcome and land a big fish.

Your tactical aim is straightforward: apply as much leverage and tension as possible on the fish without breaking the tippet. Leverage is the pressure you apply to the fish to try to control its direction, while tension is the

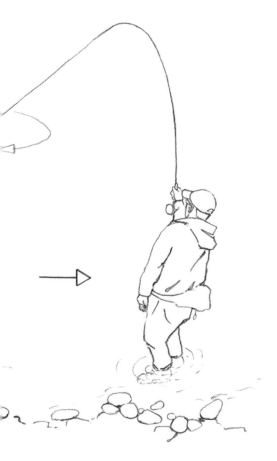

amount of stress you place on the leader, line, and rod.

Whenever possible, hold your rod directly above the fish and remain as close to the fish as you can. This usually results in the angler chasing the fish upstream and down, taking in line whenever possible and keeping the rod tip high above the fish. Maintaining a short line—preferably one to three rod lengths between you and the trout—decreases the chances of the trout taking control of the fight.

To help my clients understand this technique, I use the example of walking a dog. In this case you are trying to keep the dog on a short leash and next to you during your walk. This way you can keep control of your dog and be able to react if it runs or misbehaves. This also applies to trout: You want to stay as close to the fish as possible during the fight so that you have more control and influence.

AUTHOR'S TIP

If you are not able to stay close to the fish and put leverage directly above its head, place your rod tip at an extreme sideways angle while remaining perpendicular with the trout. This helps you keep control and maintain pressure on the giant during the fight.

When a big fish runs some distance away from you, it decreases your ability to put upwards or sideways leverage on it. The risk of losing it is greatly increased. Plus, by staying close, you avoid the additional tension created by the drag of the line through the water, and you can use your rod to steer the line or the fish out of danger should

your line wrap around an object in the river. Your goal is to wear down the fish. Your immediate objective is to prevent it from getting its head down and using its full strength to fight you.

To generate leverage on a fish, use good rod placement to help you to direct the fish to a good spot where you can net it. Of course, the trout will try to get to fast, turbulent water where it can use its strength to the maximum. Here are some tricks that will help you stay in control, and maintain leverage on a big fish.

As soon as possible, steer the fish into shallower and slower-moving, water, by applying sideways—and slightly downstream—leverage with the rod. Some anglers like to lay the rod parallel to the water to exert side pressure, but I prefer to hold the rod at a 45-degree angle, which keeps the trout's head up and applies constant pressure. By forcing the trout downstream, you are fighting the fish, not the current it's swimming in.

To throw the fish off balance, change rod position frequently between pointing the tip skyward and applying side pressure on the fish. Such radical changes in direction of leverage disorient the fish, causing it to come to the surface and shake its head. It tires faster. When you do everything right, your big trout will start to show signs of fatigue and may even start to roll in the water as a last, frantic attempt to break free.

GUIDING TROUT AROUND STRUCTURE

I swear, at times it seems as if the trout has a pre-planned path it can travel to wrap your leader around structure. While of course this is not true, many of the trout that my friends, clients, and I have lost is a direct result of going around or into these obstacles. Trophy trout use this structure to find cover after they are hooked. They feel the pressure from the fight and they imme-

This uniquely spotted leopard rainbow was caught one wintry January day in icy, clear water. Here in the ski-crazy Rocky Mountains, many people hit the slopes on powder days—I prefer the river.

diately want to retreat from their fear that a predator is trying to get them. A large trout is strong enough to get to these shelters in the river fast and furiously.

To prevail when fighting a trophy around the structure, use your rod tip as a guide. Place the rod above the fish or as close to it as you can. Then follow the trout's movements with the rod. If it goes above the structure or below, your rod should be placed above, and in line with, the giant. Then whenever possible try to steer the fish free when it puts any distance between itself and the structure.

This will ultimately prevent your line, leader, and tippet form fraying on the structure and breaking. It also allows you to direct the fish into open water where you can fight the trout.

Another thing to remember when thinking of structure: Don't forget to include yourself or your partner as a possible target. When the fish is tiring and you are getting close to the point of netting, be

AUTHOR'S TIP

If there is too much distance between you and the fish for you to stay close and steer the fish freely around a rock or log, pinch the line with your index finger while keeping hold of your rod. Then pull out three to four feet of excess line quickly. Roll cast this extra line over and beyond the snag, causing the trout to feel pressure momentarily from the shooting line on the other side of the rock. This will direct the pressure to the other side of its jaw, sometimes fooling it into darting in the other direction and freedom. As soon as you can, regain any extra line.

Matt momentarily hoists a 10-pound rainbow before safe release. What thrill watching this trout swimming upstream with its back half out of the river. It's not every day you see such a surprise in shallow water.

careful where you are positioned, because the large trout often leaves a burst or two of energy at the end of the fight to try to break off by going through your legs or the legs of the person netting the fish.

Throughout the years, these techniques have been my saving grace. I have developed and refined these practical methods of fighting fish because I was tired of losing large trout and having my clients lose them. These strategies will add to your success on the water, whether you have been fly fishing your whole life, or are just starting out in this awesome sport. It boils down to two simple words: Take control. You'll increase your odds at landing that trout of a lifetime.

This bad boy was a sight for sore eyes in a rain-swollen tributary clouded with marginal visibility. I fished a bright red Copper John nymph in hopes that a fish would see my fly in the stained water. He did.

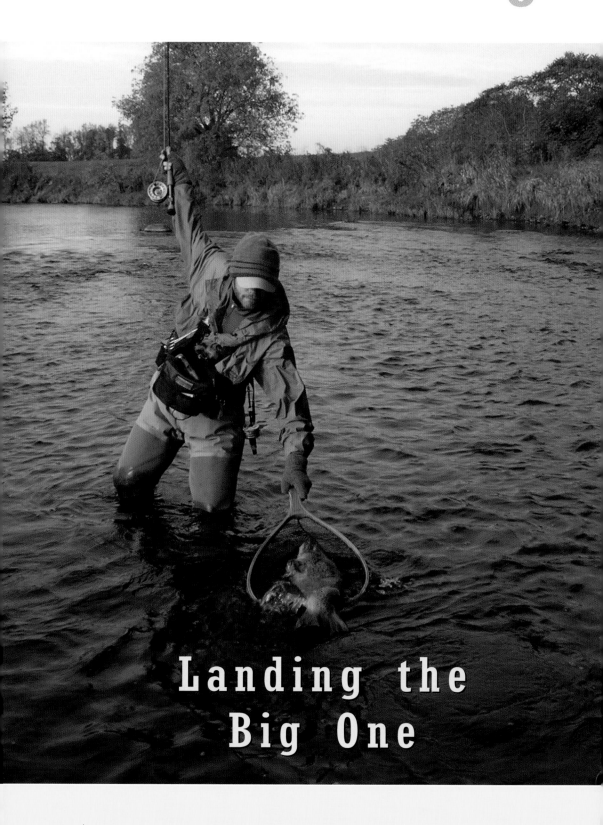

CHAPTER 8

Landing the Big One

SOMETIMES WE HAVE TO LEARN THE HARD WAY. This story is painful for me to tell because I am forced to relive such a depressing incident. However, this experience taught me some valuable lessons. Because of what I learned I have landed more trophies since.

It was one of the coldest days I had encountered while fishing for large rainbow trout. It was early February and the highs for the day were forecast to reach 5–10°F. The ride to the river was exhausting. What is normally a three-hour drive turned into six hours because of the persistent snowstorm. I enjoy days like this because it adds to the adventure of the trip and typically results in great fishing. We finally arrived at the river and stepped outside the vehicle.

"Man, it's freezing out here!" I said. With each breath I felt my lungs burning deep down. But this is the price you pay to catch the trout of your life.

The water was low and ultra clear. We could see every little detail in the water. This area is known for huge snowfalls; the six- to seven-foot snowdrifts lining the river confirmed that. I was fishing with a couple of my fishing partners. Their enthusiasm for fly fishing is contagious and I thought this trip would only add more fuel to their fire. As we started our journey upstream, we soon realized it was going to be a long trek. Every few steps we took, we sank up to our waist in snow. "I hope you brought your snowshoes," one of them said jokingly.

"That wouldn't be a bad idea today," I said. We finally made it upstream to a section of water known to hold trophy trout— or, as I like to call them, the "big dogs." Matt, who is experienced in catching trophy trout, stayed downriver and was exploring stretches of his favorite water.

As we continued, I noticed a wake from a fish darting upstream in a fairly calm section of the river. Before I could point it out, my buddy shouted, "Oh, my God, look at that wake, that fish must be huge!"

"Right on," I replied. "That's what we came here for. Duck down."

I thought we had spooked the fish; maybe that's why it was darting upstream. We watched the wake until it stopped. Then, in the deep snow, we crept up slowly and clumsily on the giant snow banks. As we got to a point where we could cast to the fish, my body was shaking. I knew that whoever was going to cast to this fish had only a few shots. It was so bitterly cold that the ice would clog the rod tips instantly, and changing the flies we put on at the car was out of the question.

We got into position. We could see an enormous red gill plate of a huge buck rainbow. I looked at my buddy and said, "This is the one, I'm sure it is at least the 20-pounder I've been looking for."

He then looked at me and said, "Get 'em, man—show me how it's done." I pulled out enough line to make the cast, which was very difficult because I was perched high on the snow bank and I had to compensate the line length by seven or eight feet to make the cast. *Well, it's now or never,* I thought before my cast.

I released the line to a spot upstream from the fish where the flies would have time to sink and drift into the trout's feeding lane.

"Oh, man, I'm short," I said as my flies entered the water. Just then the buck turned to the left, opened his huge jaws, and took the fly. My heart went to my throat. I set on surely the largest trout I had seen to date.

After a few intense headshakes, the fish bolted. Despite the thick snow, I gave chase. I had to be extremely careful how much pressure I applied on the 6x tippet. I immediately realized that being high above the hooked trout was an advantage because of the pressure I could apply to its jaw.

After a good fight, I finally whipped the fish and it was time to try to get the big boy in the net. By this time, my other fishing partner, seeing and hearing all the commotion, came over to the river's edge ready to net the monster. Because the banks were so high, the only way to get to the river's edge was to sit on my butt and slide down. My two fishing companions followed with nets in hand. One of my fishing partners along on this trip lacked experience with large trout. His eagerness to land this fish and see first hand what true trophy trout looks like up close led to the devastating outcome.

As part of my fish-fighting strategy, I turned the tired fish sideways to the edge of the river and into the slowest water I could find. By this time, the fish was near the surface, lying on its side and protesting with feeble headshakes every few seconds.

"He's ready," I said.

The momentarily tired fish was downstream from my fishing partner who was closest to the fish. I had to rely on him to do the job before the rainbow got a second wind and headed downstream to a stretch of river choked with debris. At that moment it happened: Instead of keeping his net in the water and letting the fish slide in head first, he lunged at the fish from above.

Not having time to say anything and knowing this could be the end of the fight, I gripped my rod firmly, closed my eyes, and…tink! The fish broke the tippet. My worst fears unfolded right in front of me.

While attempting to scoop the fish, my buddy had hit my leader and tippet with his net. Once the huge trout felt relief from the pressure that had it tethered, it mustered a last burst of energy and got away. Just then he looked up at me with profound sadness and said, "I'm so sorry man!" I knew he was sincere and felt really bad. I accepted some of the blame. I also said, "This is a great experience—you can't land them all."

The ride home that night was long. But in the end the pros outweighed the cons in this sad experience. Furthermore, it helped increase our collective knowledge of what to do—and what not to do—when trying to net the trout of a lifetime.

Getting a large trout in the net can be the hardest part of the process, and potentially, the most heartbreaking. At the end of the fight, when the fish detects you or the net in the water, count on it erupting in a final explosion. Don't get overly eager and try to drag the fish back toward you or apply undo pressure on the line to keep the fish from running. Impatience at this stage can be disastrous.

You want to control the fight until the fish is safely in the net, so don't hurry and never try to net a fish in fast current. Watch how the fish acts to determine if it is ready. If you attempt to net a fish too soon, you stand a good chance of breaking your tippet with the rim of the net. If a fish rolls on the surface or can no longer hold its position in the current and starts to swim downstream, you're in business. If you are applying the accurate amount of pressure during the fight, you can land these beasts in short time without hurting the trout.

There's nothing like early-season chrome. The challenge was staying close to the cart-wheeling aerial show.

Notice the extension Angus gets when netting this trophy. Such a reach cushions the tippet from breaking.

ALWAYS net the fish head first. This ensures that any last burst will propel the fish into the net, not away from it. It is important that you are focused. Don't attempt to net the fish too early or tail first. Stay calm, continue to use and practice these techniques, and you'll land more and larger trout with ease.

I always get a kick out of watching some anglers and their buddy's trying to net large trout when in chest-deep water. The trout gets wrapped around their leg and they don't even know it until its too late. Just remember don't chase the fish, direct it into reasonable water, and then net it.

Hooked trout behave fairly predictably. Recognizing when the fish is nearing the end of the fight—and looking around to quickly find the proper conditions around you for landing it— allows you to successfully net the fish without overplaying it.

RATTLE AND ROLL

When a large trout is hooked, the most common reaction is a series of violent headshakes, the *"rattle"*. This action is an attempt to dislodge the fly from its mouth, and to try to relieve the pressure it's feeling from the tension you're applying with the rod. The fish will expend much energy during these headshakes, which is a tactical and effective way to tire the fish quickly.

Many anglers believe that the runs or quickened rushes a fish make during the fight tire the fish. The fact is that when a fish runs, it is routinely propelling its tail in a forward movement, but at a faster pace. In contrast, when a fish goes into headshakes, it is using its entire body at attempting to get away. This not only saps a lot of energy from the fish, it is also an unnatural movement that causes the fish to go upside down and "roll" while shaking. This unbalances the fish for a few seconds until it gains its equilibrium.

Stay attuned to the fish's every move. This small window of imbalance is an opportunity to net the fish, because the fish is virtually unable to right itself and dart away from the net. Be alert for these conditions and act instantly. Once the fish regains balance and its bearings, you can count on it resuming an aggressive fight. Don't rush things, if you miss this window of opportunity, keep fighting and watch for signs of tiring.

The fish thinks it's fighting for its life. The strength of the fish when you're fighting it confirms this.

Headshakes and rolling just below the surface of the water are the signature moves of a hooked trout. The difference in these actions at the end of the fight is that the movements are slower and take longer for the fish to perform. They also cause the fish to become unbalanced for a longer period of time. There are two ways to take advantage of these actions.

When the fish rolls below the surface and is unbalanced; position your rod with sideways pressure toward the bank you are standing on or near. This allows you to turn the fish, guiding it toward shallower water and a waiting net. It also allows you to gain more control throughout the fight, helping ensure you have more chances to get into position to net the fish.

The second advantage is the opportunity to net the fish—but be careful. Netting the fish in this situation is risky. The fish is just below the surface and can easily make a bolting run if it regains its balance. If you are fighting a trophy, you may want to be a little more patient. Try landing the fish when conditions are more predictable, or if you can obviously see that the fish is clearly unbalanced, and you are close to the fish and have your net ready. If that is the case, quickly net the fish, but remember to do it head first.

READY FOR THE NET

Toward the end of the fight when you have started tiring the fish out, it occasionally turns and rolls on the surface. Momentarily it begins drifting back with the current. This is the best indication that the fish is ready to be netted.

When the fish turns or rolls on the surface of the river, it has once again become unbalanced. Before it regains balance, it is your opportunity to land the fish. The fish is momentarily immobilized and you can ease it into the net. It's important to react fast. Net the fish as soon as it starts to turn and roll on the surface, this will ensure you don't overplay or hurt the fish.

Don't overplay or exhaust this fish, as this can be deadly for the fish. If you clearly see signs of the fish becoming exhausted, quickly net the fish, remove the fly, and start reviving the trout as soon as possible.

AUTHOR'S TIP

When the trout starts to drift with the current, place yourself down stream of the fish and use the current to your advantage. Let drift the trophy to your net.

I have never had a fight with a large trout that is the same as the one before. I fundamentally know what expect and have a good idea on the sequences, but there is always something I encounter that is unpredictable. I've hooked fish that have fought me hard and have tested me every minute of the fight, whereas there are some that have been over in as little as one or two minutes.

I recall a fish I hooked in the shallow riffles one late spring. I could tell the fish was big, its behavior was very aggressive. It was in water that had an even depth. The fish was suspended, and suspended trout are usually feeding trout. It only took half a dozen drifts before I hooked this trophy, I knew I had my hands full. So I tried to relax, as much as is possible in this situation, and prepared myself for a super-intense battle. Little did I know this would be one of the shortest fights I had experienced!

The fish took and I set the hook, and the fish immediately leaped out of the water in a spray of frenzied headshakes. I anticipated a terrific run to follow, but once the fish landed back in the water, it continued thrashing on the surface. Maybe 10 seconds elapsed and I realized I might be able to net this fish. I reached my net out just below the fish. While it was thrashing about, the current pushed the fish right into the net. I couldn't believe it.

My fishing partner had been videotaping that day and I could hear him laughing out load.

"I can't believe what I just saw," he said. "If people see this, they are going to think this stuff is easy as pie."

I joined in the laughter and asked, "How long do you think that was?"

"I don't know, maybe 30 seconds."

Later that night I watched the footage of the fight. To my surprise, it lasted only 39 seconds—still unbelievable. Clearly, the key to this quick fight was my understanding of the fish's reactions and my swift reaction. The prize was a gorgeous eight-pound, brightly colored rainbow. The fish that gave up so soon will stay in my mind for many trout to come.

Reading when the fish is disoriented or off balance allows you to seize the moment and avoid that last burst trout are so often known for just before being netted. It also gives you a better understanding of where to position yourself and the net.

Devout fly fisher John Garrett displays a beautiful rainbow caught on a cool spring day.

To effectively net a trophy trout without too much fuss or thrashing, always scoop the fish head first. This ensures that the trout ends up in the net if it has a sudden burst of energy. Position your rod hand behind you at an upward 45-degree angle. Then reach out with the net in the opposite hand. This will give you adequate reach to be effective, while allowing you to reposition your arm if the trout runs. Always position yourself down stream from the trout using the river's current to your advantage.

GETTING INTO POSITION

Getting yourself into position when you preparing to net your trophy is a critical step in the process. Too many times I have seen anglers chasing the fish with their net during the fight, which usually leads to fish breaking off.

If you are fighting a fish and in deep water, the fish will make attempts to run around or in between your legs. It is not doing so to make it hard for you to net it. The fish simply sees your legs as structure in the water and uses it to try to break free. So keep your legs together.

Another thing to remember is if you are chasing the fish around with your net during the fight, you are losing concentration on fighting the fish and applying the right amount of pressure when it is needed. This can cause you to overplay and hurt the fish, not to mention increase your chances of breaking off your trophy.

AUTHOR'S TIP

Keep the net half in the water and be prepared to move the net to either side in case the fish makes a dash at the last minute.

As you are nearing the end of the fight and contemplating netting the fish, it is recommended that you are downstream of the fish and that you are able to react quickly. Try not to lunge at the fish, which can spook the fish into doing a final run. Stay calm and when you have placed the net into position below the fish, you then want to apply pressure from your rod to lift the fish's head up. This is best accomplished by keeping the rod in an upward and slightly horizontal position, then extending your arm at an upward angle behind and away from your body. This will give you the ability to reach forward and get extra extension with the net.

It is helpful to keep your body pointed toward the fish when attempting to net it, just in case you need to make adjustments if the fish does a last minute run. By keeping your rod positioned slightly horizontal, it will allow the rod the ability to absorb the pressure without reaching the breaking point. Ensuring you the chance of landing the fish of a lifetime.

I know that this part of the fight can seem to simple to worry about. Personally, I think that is a common mistake made by many anglers. Some just don't realize they are netting the fish wrong, they are too eager in the moment and would rather try to power the fish in.

I learned the hard way with one of the largest trout I have ever hooked, so now I am very conscious when the time comes to land the fish I am fighting. The next time you are in the act of landing that trout of your life concentrate on the trout's movements and use these techniques to land that trophy.

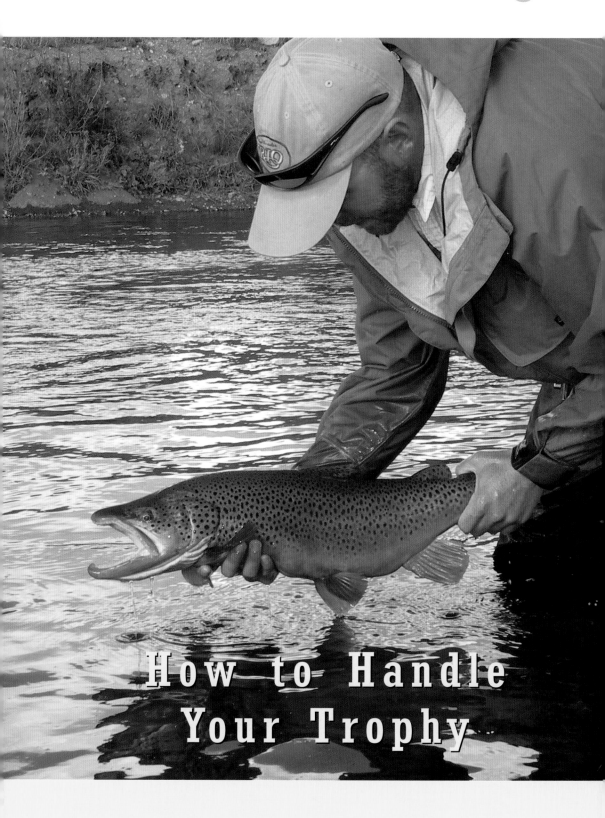

CHAPTER 9

How to Handle Your Trophy

THE PICTURE IS PERFECT. You've landed the trout of your dreams. It's late afternoon and everything bathed in rich, alpenglow light. Your fishing partner has the right angle with your smiling face in the photo—you and your empty hands. You've dropped the fish. Suddenly you look like Rocky Balboa when he screams out "Adrienne!"

We've all been there: The trout is big and strong and slippery. It's hard to hold onto a live creative in fear of pending execution. It doesn't realize all you have in mind is an innocent photo op. While capturing this smiling moment in a lasting picture of happiness is important to you, so is the fish's well being. This chapter will help ensure that the next trophy you land enjoys his part of the ending.

Understanding how to handle a trophy during the heart-pounding excitement of landing your fish-of-a-lifetime is as important as knowing how to catch such a prize. Following through competently will give you the satisfaction of seeing this wonderful creature live to fight another day. Performing this last stage of the whole process surely and swiftly will ensure the big trout's full recovery.

There are likely a number of things you want to do once you have landed your big fish—pictures, weighing, measuring, admiring your catch, catching your breath, and simply relishing the glowing moment. Stop! The essential thing to remember above all else is to *keep the fish in the water between pictures and when measuring length and girth.* Keeping your fish in your net and in the water keeps it both securely captive and safe. Make certain the water is deep enough to accommodate easy breathing for the fish—its gills should be working steadily. Also choose water clear of debris and mud.

Once the fish is netted, your first step is to remove the fly from its mouth. Follow these common sense guidelines when handling a large trout leading up to its careful release:

Always wet your hands before touching the fish. Trout have a protective membrane coating that helps protect them. Their lateral line is particularly sensitive. If a fish is handled with non-lubricated hands, you risk removing the vital protective coating, which can damage the fish making them susceptible to bacteria growth or even kill the fish.

When holding a trout, try to handle it gently, without squeezing too hard, as this can cause internal damage to the fish. What I have realized is that if you have an aggressive grip, the trout will work even harder to free itself. If the trout starts to squirm, release some pressure and place the fish in the water for a few seconds, preferably within your net, just in case you loose your grip. Instinctively, you will want to squeeze harder if the trout starts to squirm, but the reality is that if you release pressure, the trout will almost always calm down.

I have seen it too many times: the angler is holding his trophy and the fish moves—his reaction is to quickly try to grip the fish tightly. The trout will shoot up in the air like a missile. What a cluster this situation can turn into. While in the moment there is some humor to witnessing this, it is damaging to the trout and if the trout is handled correctly this will not happen to you. Cradle your trophy by cupping one hand and holding it under the fish, just behind the front fin, and with your other hand, grip the trout near the tail. This is not only a healthy way to hold a trout; it also makes for an awesome picture!

Always balance the fish when handling it. Keep it in the same position it would be in the water. There are three major mistakes that are sometimes made when a trout is being handled:

Picking the trout up by the mouth. This could break the trout's jaw, causing it to be detached and affecting its ability to eat, usually resulting in death.

Picking the fish up by the gills. This limits its ability to obtain oxygen, potentially damaging or killing the fish.

Picking the fish up by the tail. This can cause the fish to bend its body unnaturally and the uneven amount of weight from the rest of its body will internally damage the fish.

Measure the length and girth of the fish while it's still submerged in the water. Performing these tasks when the fish is submerged will allow it to begin the reviving process quickly.

When taking pictures, hold the trout out of the water for only a few seconds, and then allow a longer period of time for the fish to "catch its breath" underwater before lifting him out where he can't breathe for another shot. This will also help the fish revive.

It is very easy to get caught up in the moment when you have just landed a trophy trout. The excitement and adrenaline rush can cause you to lose sight of one of the most important steps in catch and release, the reviving stage. Plus it doesn't help when your fishing partner is there in the excitement with you drooling over your shoulder, yelling out "that fish is a pig!"

During a great fight, the trout builds up lactic acid and becomes very exhausted. It is imperative to help the trout recover quickly by handling the fish as little as possible and to get the trophy back in the water, preferably in an area where there is an ample supply of oxygen. As I am nearing the end of a good fight with a strong trout, I remind myself of this important step so that I ensure a successful recovery.

Once I have landed a trophy, I remove the fly and keep it in my net, submerged in debris-free water until I am ready to take a picture or to admire the fish. By concentrating first on the fish, I remember to take care of the trout's vital needs and then shift the focus on getting prepared for that perfect snapshot. This requires understanding how to keep the trout safe and healthy. Avoiding misguided rough handling of a superior fish makes for a healthy happy ending to a great battle. This not only ensures the safety of your individual trophy, but also gives it an excellent chance to swim away and create future generations of fighting, wild trout.

CAPTURING THE MOMENT

Position your fishing companion (or yourself, if you are the photographer) exactly before you take the picture. Compose the shot in advance, without the fish. Okay, now lift the fish quickly and gently press the shutter, all in one clean motion. Once the shot is taken, immediately put the fish back in the water before taking another one. Between each shot, begin reviving the fish. Give it time to breathe. *Never* put the fish on the bank or keep it out of the water while you are making its portrait. And take it easy, two or three well-focused pictures are plenty to capture the moment.

THE REVIVING

I like to define the term "reviving" as the way to allow a trout to regain its

Patience is a winning strategy with big trout. Brian Strickland had to wait for this giant to move into a shaded run to feed. I like to refer to this yellow beauty as a banana brown—wild trout don't come much prettier.

Rule number one: get the fish in quickly. Then, in reviving your trophy for release, always hold the trout upright and into the current so it gets the oxygen it needs to regain its energy and lives to see another day.

strength and oxygen supply lost during the fight. This is a crucial step. If not carried out correctly, the fish will not survive. However, this is an excellent opportunity to admire the magnificent giant you have just landed—you just want to be sure that the revival of the fish is your top priority.

Trout build up lactic acid in the blood and muscles after a hard fight, this exhausts the trout physically and requires them to gain back their strength. It is similar to us going to the gym and doing a hard cardio work out then needing protein and rest to replenish your muscles from fatigue. The trout will remove the lactic acid build up by picking up dissolved oxygen through their gills. Their are two ways the trout can obtain this oxygen:

The first way is by opening their mouth and gathering the oxygen then closing their mouth and force it through there gills.

The second way is by keeping their mouth open and extending their gills allowing the oxygen to pass through while swimming up stream.

It has been common practice for many years that the correct way to revive a fish for release is to gently rock the fish back and forth, presumably giving it oxygen. While this can be done successfully, it can also be misleading. What I mean is that just because the fish slowly swim away from you it doesn't mean it won't go belly up a few minutes later from lack of oxygen. This can result from the unnatural flow of water through the fish's gills when it is rocked back. This will actually disable the fish from circulating the full amount of dissolved oxygen through its gills and not allow it to regain some much needed strength.

I have found that the best way to revive a trophy is to cradle the trout with two hands and position the fish upstream, allowing the current to deliver the oxygen directly to the fish. Hold the fish in faster turbulent water if possible. Try to keep the fish as horizontal as possible—and try not to squeeze it very hard when handling it. This will allow the fish to naturally circulate water through its gills, allowing it to get the full amount of oxygen and regaining its strength. You can also add to the process by splashing your hand in the water above the fish, thus increasing the amount of dissolved oxygen flowing into the trout's bloodstream.

AUTHOR'S TIP

If you are fishing with a partner, have them stand upstream to cause a break or seam in the water. Once the water is clear of debris, cradle the fish and place it facing upstream in the newly created seam, which creates additional oxygen in the water and helps the trout recover more rapidly.

Keep the fish positioned upstream and fully submerged. Hold the fish in this position until it swims away from your hands energetically. This pretty well guarantees that the fish has been released successfully.

To me, there is no greater satisfaction in fly fishing than watching a wary fish you have worked so hard for, swim away alive and well, with the knowledge it will live to fight another day. Not only is momentarily capturing such an exceptional trout exhilarating, and cradling it gratifying, you know that your enjoyment did not lead to this fish's demise. That's what catch and release is all about.

Throughout the years and countless days on the water, I have witnessed a number of trout being mishandled by anglers.

I love the element of surprise when targeting browns in the fall; sometimes I get the bonus of a rainbow.

Did you know that each "spot" on a brown trout is made up of three connecting spots?

However, there is one incident that always comes to mind. It was the end of a perfect day while fishing some great catch and release water with two clients—great fishing, clear skies, and no wind. I was packing up the gear and saying farewell when I heard someone hollering. I looked towards the river and saw an angler running near the river's edge yelling to his partner, "Get the camera, get the camera!" Just then I had a bad feeling and realized that the trout the angler had just landed was not in the water, instead it was on the bank flopping around. I ran to towards where the fish was, crossed the river, and picked up the magnificent brown trout, approximately 6lbs. I immediately placed this awesome fish in the river and tried desperately to revive it. The giant brown was exhausted from the fight and from being out of the water, I did everything I could to try resuscitate it. Reviving the fish failed and the big brown died. Just then the angler returned with his camera and wanted me take his picture with the fish. I refused and proceeded to tell the angler for the following five minutes about proper etiquette and how to properly care for, and release, a trophy trout. It was truly a sad ending to what should have been a perfect day.

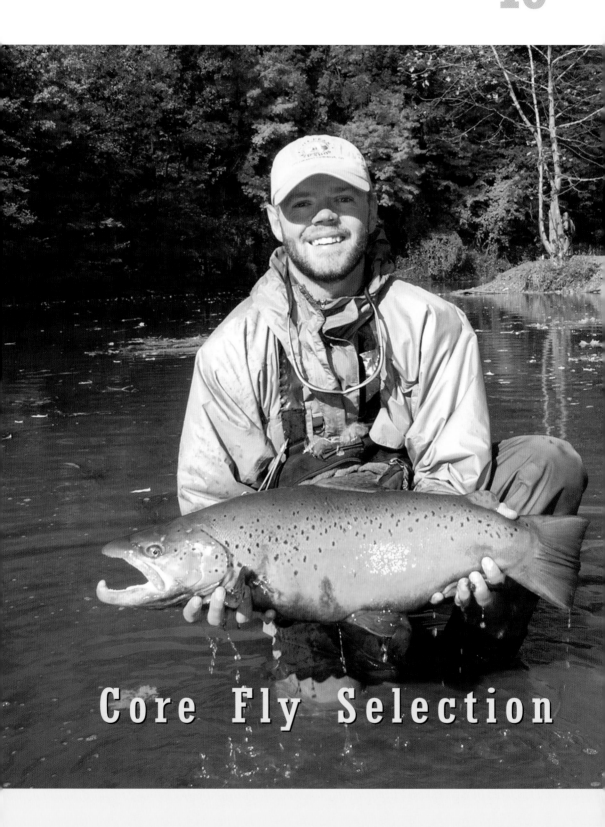

Core Fly Selection

WHEN I SHOW SOMEONE A PICTURE of an impressive trout that I've recently caught, I wish I could make $5 by betting on the first question…"What did you catch it on?" It's nearly inevitable.

While the answer is occasionally interesting—and might even be useful information for fishing a specific season or river—it is far from the most revealing strategically.

The fly on the end of my leader doesn't catch the big one, I catch the big one. There, I've said it. How you present the fly has more to do with your success than the choice of fly. While choosing the correct fly will defiantly help you catch the fish, it's not as crucial as the steps leading up to the trophy seeing your fly.

Your success with trophy trout depends almost entirely on how well you present the fly to the fish. Because large trout are opportunistic feeders, they rarely pass up a meal, especially when the meal is high in protein and alluring in size. Such prey is worth expending energy since it exceeds the nutritional value the fish would otherwise ingest by eating numerous smaller insects. With this in mind, the most effective combination when searching for giant trout is to determine the primary or best food supply for the fish and imitate it with the best presentation possible. In my experience, if the fly is presented properly, nine out of 10 times, the fish will take it.

Okay, I admit that I enjoy throwing streamers—there's nothing like the raw sensation of a solid attack strike on the strip. There are times that I've almost had the damn rod ripped out of my hand.

By the way, here is a great tip that increases the odds when fishing streamers. My good friend John Barr introduced me to this double-streamer technique using his killer streamer pattern, the Slump Buster, which in this case he calls "Double Slumps." Like all of John's patterns, it lives up to its billing.

I can still see John's first cast into the head of long riffled run on the productive Yampa River—*slam*. "Fish on!" I knew John had a good fish on. Well after hooking into the beast, his rod was doubled over and he could hardly budge it.

A few minutes later he hollered, "Landon, I think he's ready for the mesh." I discreetly slid this chunk of chrome muscle into the net and looked up at John: "Are you kidding me—your first cast and, WHAM, an eight pounder?" *Unreal*, I thought, but John had instantly confirmed that the two-streamer rig was too irresistible to at least one of the biggest fish in the run.

I like to think of trophy trout as compulsive eaters. From attacking small fry on the river's edge to sucking down emergers by the hundreds, their main goal is eating whenever and whatever possible. In this chapter I'll discuss the foods preferred by trophy trout and explain how these animals live and survive in a variety of water conditions.

Food is the fuel that propels the fish to grow large; food is what maintains their

Here's John Barr with the Yampa River chromer that charged his deadly Slump Buster streamer.

giant proportions. The following is a basic list of high-protein, quality food supplies that are the main contributors to a giant trout's size.

Still, there's the unavoidable question: What did you catch him on? I promise: Later on in this chapter, to help ease the mystery of selecting flies for big trout, I'll list my top favorite patterns. These are the flies I am never without when fishing for trophy trout—Core Selection.

First, though, let's look at what really matters: choice foods that exceptionally large trout cannot resist.

SCUDS

The scud is a freshwater crustacean inhabiting many of the waters holding trophy trout. This is no accident. Their range of suitable habitat is diverse. Abundant populations of scuds are found in natural lakes, man-made reservoirs, spring creeks, and coldwater tailrace streams below dams. Generally speaking, in a reservoir with a substantial population of scuds, it would not be uncommon to find 40,000 to 50,000 scuds per acre.

Scuds thrive at the bottom of most waters in the vegetation. When I talk to clients about the river's basic entomology, I randomly pick up a handful of vegetation from the river bottom. Normally there are several dozen scuds squirming around in it. The anglers quickly get the picture why this is a huge part of the trout's diet.

While in the water, scuds swim or move with their bodies straight and positioned sideways. The crustaceans feed on dead plant and animal matter and are one of the foremost sources of protein for trout in fresh water.

When fishing scuds, the most important thing to realize is that when a scud swims, it is natural shape is straight. Only out of the water do they appear humped or curved. So when you're tying or selecting flies to imitate a living scud, for the sake of accuracy, make sure the imitation has a relatively straight profile. The second thing to keep in mind is their coloration, which is commonly tan olive or gray. Live scuds come in various shades of these colors. When a scud dies, their color changes to orange and its body develops a curve.

Orange scuds are most prolific in waters where the flows are routinely subject to change, sudden on-and-off water releases and consequential fluctuation in water levels. Scuds that get stuck in the rocks or vegetation when the water recedes, end up dying. When flows increase, their bodies float away with the current. Turbulent water released from the bottom of dams also kills many scuds. Of course, the trout love them, because there is no chance of the dead ones escaping, it becomes an easy meal.

The size of a scud varies from the equivalent of hook size 12 to 20. Colors vary as well. Do some aquatic research. Investigate the scuds in your trophy waters and you will enjoy greater success with these imitations.

AUTHOR'S TIP

When targeting the best time to fish scuds, the spring has been my most productive time of year. This is when most waterways see their highest flows and when scuds are frequently washed downstream in vast numbers. I am never without a scud on my rig during this time of year when fishing rivers known for a large scud population.

MYSIS SHRIMP

The mysis shrimp is another freshwater crustacean found in reservoirs and lakes throughout the country. These shrimp prefer water temperatures lower than 57°F, which drives them to dwell deep. The result in many cases is that bottom-release dams spew mysis shrimp into the tailwater discharges below their reservoirs, producing some of the world's largest trout.

The introduction of mysis shrimp has produced trout of breathtaking proportions.

Mysis shrimp are one of the richest protein supplies for trout, causing fish to grow fast and big—and I mean big. In my home state of Colorado, there are reservoirs that supply large quantities of mysis shrimp to resident river fish inhabiting these tailwaters. Some of these trout are known to grow in excess of 20 pounds. Personally, I believe there is possibility of a 30-pound trout! The thing that makes these mysis shrimp-fed trout so unique is that they don't gain this size and body proportions by traveling out to a large body of fresh water or an ocean, they simply take up permanent residence in the rivers where they were born and feed often on this rich protein supply, transforming them into beautifully colored mammoths.

I have been on the water when there are huge numbers of shrimp floating down stream and the river takes on a white tint. The trout immediately start a feeding frenzy; they feed so heavily when I land a trophy during this time they literally have coughed up a hand full of shrimp. This gives truth when referring to a large trout as a pig.

Deep-dwelling mysis shrimp have an aversion to light. During daylight hours they live in the darkest reaches of a body of water. At night they rise up in the water column to shallower depths. During winter months they spread out in various water depths because, of course, sunlight cannot penetrate the surface of the water when it's frozen. This behavior gives anglers a notable advantage because during the day when the shrimp are deep and venture too close to the face of the dam, they get sucked into the portals, often in great numbers.

Unlike other freshwater crustaceans, these shrimp are completely translucent when alive. They grow to as long as one and a half inches. When they travel through the release valves on most reservoirs, they are killed by the turbulent water, making them easy prey for trophy trout. When dead, they turn white or opaque, and in most cases, appear shredded or deformed.

White is the best color for this imitation. The size of the natural varies, although in my experience, a size 16 fly is best. Fish seldom hesitate to take it. My favorite conditions for using these patterns is when the flows are higher and as a result, more shrimp are released and washed downstream. So if there is a rise or sudden

---

AUTHOR'S TIP

To best imitate a mysis shrimp on a certain river, you should first determine if the shrimp floating downstream are dead or alive. I base this off of how turbulent the water is coming out of the dams release valve. If the water is ripping out, I know the shrimp will be dead and white in color. If the release is fairly calm and less turbulent, I surmise the shrimp have a chance to survive and possess a translucent body. This should help you select the appropriate shrimp imitation.

release into these waterways, don't miss out because most of these shrimp will die when entering the river. You will find the highest concentration to be right below the damn to about a mile downstream. Since the mysis shrimp are dead, the concentration of the food source is relatively close to the area where they are released. Find the food and you find the fish, ready to eat.

SOW BUGS

Found in many of the same places you find scuds, these freshwater crustaceans feed on dead or decaying vegetation and also inhabit the dark areas in and between aquatic plants. The sow bug is a flat-bodied crustacean high in protein. When in the water they are in constant motion and are gray.

I fish imitations in size 16 or 18 and often trail it below a scud pattern in high water. When the flows in a river are dramatically increased, great numbers of both bugs are washed downstream. With sow bugs inhabiting many of the same waters as scuds, having them both on your rig can mean double the food and double the fun.

This pronounced-kype golden beauty was daintily sipping naturals on top, although most large trout would rather eat below the surface than come up. I like to trail a Barr's Emerger below my dry fly.

SCULPINS

Sculpins are bottom-dwelling fishes that inhabit both tailwater and freestone rivers in the United States. Sculpins have long been known among anglers going after big trout. And for good reason: They move slowly and offer a real mouthful for a trophy trout.

Because growing trout begin eating fish after reaching the age of three, in many sculpins quickly become a staple in their diet.

Sculpins take on the appearance and coloration of the bottom of the river they reside. To be effective in imitating sculpin, you need to incorporate the colors of the bottom of the river for the fly. The profile of the sculpin is wide and fat at the head and tapers to a tail and lower body, with large pectoral fins. They are actually one of the ugliest freshwater species. I'm reminded of the bobblehead dolls when I see a sculpin— you know, the ones where the head is three times larger than the body. Sculpins have some of the same hideous features. This little fish with a large head and a small, slender body is not going to win any beauty contests, but that doesn't seem to matter to a hungry trout.

Because sculpins spend their lives scurrying about the river bottom, I recommend you weight your imitations around the head with lead wire or a heavy core bead. I per-sonally prefer to tie my sculpin imitations long and fat, two to three inches in length, and use heavy tungsten coneheads to achieve the fat- head effect. It also gets them deep.

Fish your sculpin flies on a full-sinking or sink-tip line. A slow retrieve, keeping the fly on or near the bottom, produces results. Find out if sculpins inhabit your favorite river. A diligently fished fly will entice the biggest fish.

CRAYFISH

Although popular as sustenance and bait for smallmouth bass, crayfish are probably one of the primary trout foods most overlooked by anglers. These freshwater members of the lobster family inhabit many reservoirs and rivers, where they provide an aquatic bounty of hearty meals for notably large trout.

Fishing rivers and the inlets of many lakes, I have landed trout absolutely stuffed with crayfish. When I picked up the fish out of the water, I could feel the hard shells in their bellies. On numerous occasions I have witnessed trophy trout cough up a handful of sizeable crayfish after being netted.

Adult crayfish which grow to five inches or longer are most active in the evening hours, while juveniles are most active during the day. Young crayfish range from one to three inches in length. The shorts seem to be preferred by trout, perhaps because they are not as skilled as adults in escaping, and perhaps also because they are easier to crunch and digest.

Crayfish feed on snails, insect larvae, vegetation, and aquatic worms. They are bottom crawlers. When threatened, they flick their tails, propelling themselves backwards for a fast escape. The only time they are constantly in motion is when they are escaping. Depending on the background of their habitat, they range in color from sand yellow to olive to rusty brown.

When imitating crayfish, use a size 8 or 10 hook with lots of beading to get it deep, preferably tied with the hook facing up so you can drag it along the bottom without getting snagged. Again, same as with sculpins, heavy lines or sink-tip lines work best. You want to get your fly to the bottom fast. The most effective retrieve is a long, very slow strip punctuated with an occasional fast strip. This makes the imitation look as if it's swimming naturally and, every now and then, as if it's escaping from a predator. The getaway frequently triggers the strike.

There are a great many crayfish imitations out there tied with claws extending from the front of the fly. While these patterns can sometimes work and look reasonable when compared to a stationary crayfish, they do not resemble the animal when it feels threatened and is in normal backward motion.

When crayfish flee, their bodies are streamlined, with their claws in front of their body in a crossed position. When they move their bodies pulsate. This bit of information is key because it explains why the best of imitations are ones with a lot of supple material out of the front. Your fly should resemble the streamlined profile of an escaping crayfish. Using a pattern that is natural looking significantly increases your action on the water.

AUTHOR'S TIP

Before you present a crayfish pattern, make sure you are "matching the hatch." Wary trout sometimes turn down a crayfish if it is not the same color as the natural. The two most common shades are olive and rusty brown.

To fish an imitation of a crayfish properly, the best presentation is to cast parallel

Crayfish are a favorite of big fish with big appetites. More smallmouth bass anglers know this than trout anglers. Watch your fingers around this critter, however, because those claws won't let go. Trust me.

A high-water killer: One of the most overlooked sources of food for big trout is meaty cranefly larvae

across the stream, let the fly sink, and retrieve it back. This downstream presentation makes the fly look like it is escaping from the fish, not swimming toward the fish, which will happen with an upstream approach.

The time you're fishing waters where crayfish are present, don't pass up the chance at some hard-hitting action.

CRANEFLY LARVAE

Craneflies are aquatic insects common to many trophy trout waters in the United States. At their beginning stages of life, they are a favorite among large trout, particularly during high water flows or when the insects are migrating toward shore to burrow into the soil to pupate. Fish love them

for their size and tasty protein.

Cranefly larvae grow to four or five inches long. They look like a giant inchworm. When in motion, larvae extend and retract their bodies like an accordion. When fully extended, they reach extreme lengths. To truly appreciate just how long a cranefly larva can extend its body, from time to time I seine the river, find one and hold it in my hand, and then slightly rub its body with my finger. My clients or students watch in amazement as the worm gradually extends like a skinny accordion. It's quite the sight. The fascinated onlookers immediately understand how a trout can grow so large eating craneflies.

Cranefly larvae are most abundant in shallow areas along the river bank. They are washed loose of the gravel and pushed downstream when stream flow increases suddenly, making them an easy meal for trophy trout.

Color varies from stream to stream. The most common phases are brown, gray, olive, and white. When the larva is compressed it is half an inch long, but when swimming it extend several inches. Imitations are fashioned with an extended body, sometimes segmented to match the shape, movement, and color of the fly.

In the case of cranefly larvae, size does matter.

When imitating a cranefly larva, in my experience, the bigger the fly the better. Make your imitation long and fat. A trade secret I have used for years is incorporating a black head in my patterns. Essentially, your fly should look like a monster midge in the water—and I mean monster.

Hold on because the strikes can be intense.

EGGS

When trout and salmon spawn, females lay their eggs in suitable river bottom where they make a redd or indentation in the gravel, where they cover them and leave the eggs to incubate. While some fertilized eggs survive the process, many get swept downstream and become another high-protein meal for large trout.

Salmonid eggs are highly sought after

In Great Lakes rivers the migratory browns love to feast on eggs dropped by spawn-laden salmon.

by trout for their rich nutrients, and the fact that they cannot escape danger and therefore don't require much energy to consume. Eggs range in size from two to eight millimeters in diameter; trout eggs average four millimeters and salmon six.

After size, color is the most important characteristic to match when fishing an egg imitation. Salmon and trout eggs are different shades. When eggs are fresh from the female, they are translucent in color. When they have been exposed to the water for a certain period of time, they turn milky or opaque, and routinely start to change color.

I learned about eggs when guiding in Alaska— not just fishing egg imitations, but also knowing the difference in size and colors and how the egg is affected by being exposed to the water for various amounts of time.

AUTHOR'S TIP

Do not leave home without a bunch of size 8 apricot supreme-colored yarn eggs. This is the best producing egg on the planet. Day in and day out I catch more hogs on this egg than any other.

In rivers with sizeable runs of Pacific salmon, trophy trout migrate right along with the salmon, consuming their eggs during the spawn. Another thing to keep your ear to the ground for is a rise in the water levels when salmon or trout are spawning. This washes loose eggs downstream in large numbers, often triggering a feeding frenzy among the waiting trout. And, yes, trout are cannibals, greedily devouring eggs from their own kind whenever possible.

By understanding the life cycles, preferred environments, and behavior of the main food sources for trophy trout, you will better understand when and where the fish find nourishment. This will help you find a big trout and increase your chances of one committing to your fly.

Remember, trophy trout are more opportunistic feeders than average-sized trout; they must eat more to maintain their size. When pursuing trophies, a combined knowledge of their dietary habits and the proper presentation of the right imitation will put you on the path to success.

THE CORE SELECTION

To pinpoint a specific fly pattern that without fail is guaranteed to produce a trophy trout is silly. It's an impossible request for the simple reason that there are so many tasty treats available to trophy trout. Environmental conditions and species composition varies markedly from one area of the country to another, sometimes even in neighboring watersheds. You can't expect big browns in Michigan to be feeding on the same things big brown are feeding on in Montana.

Ultimately, then, it's up to you to assemble your own personal favorite core selection of flies tailored to the waters you wade. You should base your selection on careful study of whatever scientific reports are available, friendly discussions with other anglers who really know the river, and plain old hard-won experience. For that there is no substitute.

To help get you started, however, I have selected 14 fly patterns—a baker's dozen plus one—that resemble many of the different high-protein foods on which giant trout feast. I am never without these flies in my fly box. Throughout the years, they have been the source of many successful days on the river. This selection is broad enough so you can adapt it to covering the food supplies of various fisheries.

PMD FLASHBACK BARR EMERGER

HOOK: Wapsi Lighting Strike SE5 size 14–20

THREAD: 8/0 Light Cahill Ultra

TAIL: Clipped brown hackle fibers

ABDOMEN:
Wapsi Barr's Emerger dubbing

THORAX: PMD Superfine dubbing

WING CASE AND LEGS:
Pale olive hackle fibers

FLASH OVER THE WING CASE:
Mirage opal flash

BWO FLASHBACK BARR EMERGER

HOOK: Wapsi Lighting Strike SE5 size 14–22

THREAD: 8/0 iron gray Ultra

TAIL: Clipped brown hackle fibers

ABDOMEN:
Wapsi Barr's Emerger dubbing

THORAX: Adams gray Superfine dubbing

WING CASE AND LEGS:
Dun hackle fibers

FLASH OVER THE WING CASE:
Mirage opal flash

HOW TO FISH THIS FLY

Large trout take most of their meals below the surface. This basic habit makes the Barr's Emerger a deadly pattern. During a hatch of pale morning dun mayflies, when fish are selectively rising, I normally drift the fly just below the surface in front of the suspended trout. Most trophies prefer the submerged fly over a dry. This keeps the trout securely in its comfort feeding zone, out of aerial attack by predators.

HOW TO FISH THIS FLY

The Barr's emerger tailing off the adult dry fly is a deadly combination when trout are active on the surface. They frequently take the emerger over the adult because they don't have to break the surface of the water to obtain their food.

This I can attest to: These flies catch trout.

GARCIA'S ROJO MIDGE

HOOK: Tiemco 200 size 16–22

ABDOMEN:
8/0 black thread

BEAD: Extra small red glass

GILL TUFT:
Ultra Floss dental floss

RIB: Fine copper Lagartun wire

TYING THREAD COLLAR:
Bright green dyed peacock herl

HOW TO FISH THIS FLY

The key to success with a midge fly is the correct color. Start with it as your trailing pattern and change colors until you find the right one.

FLASHBACK PHEASANT TAIL NYMPH

HOOK: Tiemco 100SP-BL size 14–20 or TMC

THREAD: 8/0 rusty brown down to size 18, 10/0 rusty brown for size 20 and smaller

TAIL: Ringneck pheasant tail fibers

RIB: Fine copper wire

ABDOMEN:
Ringneck pheasant tail fibers

WING CASE:
Pearl Flashabou

LEGS: Ringneck pheasant tail fibers

THORAX: Peacock herl from the eyed quill (*Note: This is the original pattern; I use peacock Ice Dub for durability.*)

HOW TO FISH THIS FLY

The key to success using the Flashback Pheasant Tail is to determine if you should fish one with or without a bead. This is accomplished through trial and error. I have had trout take only beadheads at times, yet at other times they prefer it without a bead

V-RIB SOW BUG

HOOK: Tiemco 2488 H

THREAD: 8/0 UNI

BODY: Gray V-Rib

TAIL: Split light dun Fibetts

HOW TO FISH THIS FLY

I find more sow bugs than scuds in most trout water. A crustacean overlooked by some anglers, the irresistible combination of abundance and protein make it a favorite for trout. Fish this imitation in areas of the river where aquatic vegetation is thick—this is where the sow bugs dwell, and trophy trout know it.

LAWSON'S CONE-HEAD WOOL SCULPIN

HOOK: Tiemco 5263 3X long streamer hook size 4–10

THREAD: Light tan, olive or black to match head

HEAD: Light tan, olive or black spun wool clipped to shape in a wide profile, extending back to blend with the rabbit body (a cone can be added for weight)

PECTORAL FINS: Hen saddle hackle, pheasant rump, or partridge hackle

GILLS: Red wool or bright red Krystal chenille

BODY: Stripped rabbit wrapped over the hook shank, clipped on the sides and bottom

TAIL: Straight-cut rabbit fur strip over a few fibers of Flashabou

HOW TO FISH THIS FLY

Use a heavy sink-tip line when fishing any sculpin pattern. This gets the fly to the river bottom where these ugly little critters dwell, and keeps it deep during your retrieve.

RUST SLUMP BUSTER

HOOK: Tiemco 5263 size 2–10

THREAD: Black 70 denier UNI

TAIL/BODY/COLLAR:
Rust pine squirrel zonker strip

BODY: Rust Sparkle Braid

CONE: Copper tungsten

HOW TO FISH THIS FLY

Don't be afraid to fish a larger size Slump Buster, because the fly looks like a streamlined baitfish. Trout seldom pass up such a hearty meal. Plus you get a better hooking-angle with the bigger hook.

COPPER JOHN

HOOK: Tiemco 5262 size 10–18

THREAD: 70–140 denier depending on hook size

BEAD: Gold brass or tungsten

LEAD: 13 wraps of .010–.020 depending on hook size

TAIL: Brown goose biots

ABDOMEN:
Copper colored Ultra Wire

THORAX: Peacock herl

WING CASE:
Black Thin Skin with a strand of opal mirage flash pulled over the top (covered with epoxy)

LEGS: Mottled brown hen back

HOW TO FISH THIS FLY

One of the most attractive qualities of the Copper John is the coloration of the pattern's wire-wrapped body. This can be a huge advantage in many fishing situations—in the spring, for example, when trophy trout are used to seeing eggs, a pink or apricot-colored wire body often triggers a strike. This holds true during the summer months as well. And if fish are eating red midges during the winter, a small red Copper John is a fly the trout won't pass up.

MAYER'S KRYSTAL NYMPH

HOOK: Teimco 200R size 20–16

THREAD: 8/0 olive

TAIL/WING CASE/ LEGS:
Pearl Krystal Flash

ABDOMEN:
Olive goose biot

THORAX: Gray Ice Dub

HOW TO FISH THIS FLY

This pattern is most effective in shallow-water situations because this is an attractor fly, and the trout has only a split second to react and eat. The flash on the body excites the big ones in riffles.

LANDON'S LARVA

HOOK: Tiemco 206BL size 14–18

THREAD: 8/0 olive

ABDOMEN:
80/ olive thread under olive nymph rib (Larva Lace)

THORAX: Peacock Ice Dub

HOW TO FISH THIS FLY

This imitation of a caddisfly larva is most effective in spring and summer during high water. It produces well in riffled runs where insects are hyper-active, and the trout have to commit quickly before the food sweeps by. Remember that caddisflies are active in their subsurface environment up to one month before they hatch.

APRICOT SUPREME GLO BUG

HOOK: Tiemco 2488 (up eye) or 2487 (down eye) size 20–16

THREAD: 8/0 orange

THORAX: Apricot supreme Egg Yarn

HOW TO FISH THIS FLY

Position your egg fly trailing below a main fly. This allows it to drift freely off the bottom like a real egg awash in the current. If you are fishing an egg pattern by itself, extend the tippet length to achieve the same effect.

MAYER'S MYSIS SHRIMP

HOOK: Teimco 200R size 18–14

THREAD: 8/0 white

TAIL: White poly yarn

WING CASE: White poly yarn with overlaying pearl Flashabou

LEGS: Six to seven strands of clear rubber tentacles

ABDOMEN: White poly yarn under-wrapped with clear midge tubing

THORAX: White poly yarn

EYES: Black rubber eyes

HOW TO FISH THIS FLY

Create your mysis imitation with supple material such as marabou or ostrich herl. This adds movement to the fly which resembles the dead, torn-up body of a mysis shrimp.

CHAMOIS CRANEFLY

HOOK: Tiemco 200R size 16–12

THREAD: 8/0 cream

ABDOMEN/THORAX:
White leather chamois

OLIVE MEAT WHISTLE

HOOK: Gamakatsu 90-degree jig hook

THREAD: 140 denier olive UNI

BODY: Olive/Pearl Sparkle Braid

RIB: Brassie size chartreuse Ultra Wire

TAIL/WING:
Olive rabbit zonker strip

COLLAR: Barred pumpkinseed/green/orange Sili Legs, gold holographic Flashabou and olive marabou.

HOW TO FISH THIS FLY

Don't pass up the opportunity to fish a cranefly imitation in high flows, when they are flushed downstream in huge numbers. The trout won't pass them up.

HOW TO FISH THIS FLY

*Slow your retrieve **way down** when presenting the Meat Whistle. Crayfish move rapidly only when they are spooked. At other times they inch across the bottom.*

Gearing Up

GEAR MATTERS. As in any specialized sport, having the right tools for the job often makes the difference between success and failure. The gear you use while fly fishing, especially when going after trophies, can determine your success. Quality, well-functioning equipment is especially critical when dealing with trophy trout, because everything is often exaggerated when fighting and landing these giants. Every piece of equipment I have, from my hat to my reel, serves a purpose with every giant I encounter.

Because I've made selecting my equipment a priority, and I spend probably more than I should on it, my gear normally performs flawlessly. But there have been times when I was ready to heave it into the nearest dumpster.

Such a "dumpster moment" involved a good friend of mine. I first met Jack on a guided trip. He booked me to take him and his family to the South Platte. After talking with Jack and hearing a little about his fishing experience through his cool Texas accent, I quickly determined that he was an accomplished angler and would enjoy his day on this technical fishery.

We continued our conversation on the drive to the river, during which I learned that Jack has a wonderful personality and is a fine man. When we reached the water and it was time to suit up, I asked Jack, "Do you need a rod and reel?"

"No way," he replied with a light laugh. "I am not some rookie. I got it covered."

Good, I thought, he's ready to get down to business.

Jack finally stood at the river's edge, eager to make his first cast. I placed him in an even-moving riffled run and told him to fish this spot while I got the others situated. "Give 'em hell," I cried over my shoulder while hustling upstream to help the others. Having a client with experience is helpful when you're guiding more than one person. It allows you more time to introduce basic techniques to others with less experience.

About five minutes into my impromptu fishing clinic, I looked downstream to see Jack's rod bent. I arrived in time to help him land a decent 15-inch rainbow. "Good job, man," I said. "Get another."

"This time I'm gonna get his grandpa!" Jack replied.

A few minutes later Jack was hooked up again. Glacing back to one of the novices, he had a fish on as well. "Set!" I ordered, as a good-sized 'bow jumped clear of the water. We landed it and I thought, *What a start to a trip, three fish in 10 minutes.* I looked at Jack; his fish still wasn't in. I ran down and asked, "What's taking so long— you hook a whale?"

"I can't lift his head," he said.

Instantly I deciphered that Jack was using his 1980s click-and-palm reel, featuring no drag setting. Every time he lifted, the line released from the reel. I told Jack, "The only shot you have is to palm the reel and lay the wood to him." He did just that and to my surprise, pulled to the surface a monster brown, in the eight-pound class.

Oh, boy, we're in trouble now, I thought.

There was no room for error. With a fish of this size and no drag, we were in trouble. Jack continued his dance with the bruiser brown for few minutes and I knew who was winning.   "It's now or never," I told Jack. "Palm the reel and try to turn the fish into the shallows." If he couldn't do this, I knew we were going to overplay the fish and risk exhausting it beyond recovery.

The brown reacted with a rapid string of ferocious head shakes on the surface. On the last shake, I swear the giant turned and gave us the fin. In a flash it was over. Jack looked at me and calmly said: "Landon, that big ol' fish winked at me. I believe he was messin' with me the whole time."

We sat down on adjoining rocks. I tried to ease the pain of loosing such a big brown, but as a professional guide and Jack's new friend, I couldn't let the opportunity pass for a never-to-be-forgotten lesson about tackle. The next day Jack and I walked into to a local fly shop and asked me to help him pick out a high-quality reel. From that fateful minute forward, Jack has been a firm believer that all fly fishing should start with the proper gear. Amen.

Most anglers develop favorites over the years, and I'm no different. Nowadays there are dozens of makers of reels intelligently designed and finely crafted—on the high end you almost can't go wrong. And the best makers stand solidly behind their products if anything goes wrong. In the end it's largely a matter of personal choice. With a tip of the hat to the many excellent tackle makers not represented on my personal list, here is a short list of the gear I use, with explanations as to why I favor each piece of equipment.

• Polarized Sunglasses: Fishbones by Smith Optics—Color copper or Silver Creek brown.
• Fly Line: Rio Products 5- to 8-weight, weight-forward floating. Preferred Models—the Nymph Line and the Accelerator.
• Leaders: Rio Flourflex leader and tip-

pet material, both in fluorocarbon
vFly Rods: Sage fast-action models XP, Xi2, and TCR for 5- to 8-weight lines.
• Reels: Ross Cimmaron 2, Cimmaron Large Arbor, and Evolution, weights 4 to 6.
• Net: Signature Concepts or Brodin— as large as possible yet easy to carry and handle.
• Scale: Chatelaine—brass, spring-loaded, 30-pound range.
• Camera
• Long bill/ large-brimmed hat

THE EYES HAVE IT

Without question, the most important tool I have when I'm on the water is a quality pair of polarized sunglasses. Most anglers understand that the polarization of the lens takes the glare off the surface of the water, allowing you better visibility. But more important, it opens the possibility for visual fly fishing in all disciplines: dries, nymphs, streamers. This added acuity adds dimension to my performance on the water, and literally provides a new outlook in watching these magnificent creatures behave in their environment. I owe much of what I know about trout behavior to going to school through my polarized glasses.

I get a kick out of being on the water with my clients. "You see that fish?" I ask. "Cast above two or three feet and let it drift." Nine times out of 10 their response is: "Where? I can't see a thing."

I particularly enjoy what normally follows because it makes a sight-fishing believer out of nearly all. I tell the angler to continue: "Keep casting. He'll eat." I know he's questioning if there is even a fish there. And sometimes I'll get the joking response, "You probably just have me casting to a rock!" He has to rely completely on my eyes, and trust in me that a fish actually is there.

"Fish on!" This is what I love about

guiding. The ghost he was casting to is suddenly a live and thrashing trout. The angler begins an awesome journey of sight fishing for trout, with no need to convince him of the important of investing in a quality polarized glasses.

When choosing a proper pair of sunglasses for freshwater fly fishing, the key element is the tint of the lens. The best all-around colors are copper or brown. These colors lighten the water you are looking in and intensify the blues, greens, reds, and oranges—the marking of the fish you are searching for.

For extremely low-light fishing conditions, such as early mornings, late afternoons, and dark overcast days, a light amber-colored lens lightens up the water noticeably. On the other hand, for exceptionally bright conditions or light reflected off the surface of the water, such lighter-tinted lenses are not as effective. This is when a gray-shaded lens performs best. It allows you to darken the light or glare when searching for a trophy. A mirrored lens helps deflect glare off your lenses and allow you more visibility in brighter conditions.

When choosing the right shades for your home water, think about the weather—how many sunny days you typically get in a year, and the characteristics of the streams you are fishing—before you determine which lenses suit you. If you are serious about the sport and fish often, you may find it most useful to purchase more than one pair of fishing glasses so you are always prepared for a variety of weather conditions.

WHAT'S MY LINE?

Six years ago I became a basic certified casting instructor for the Federation of Fly Fishers. In preparation for my certification, I learned a great deal about what goes in to

I measure my trout in the water to prevent damaging the fish. *Whoa*—this trophy is almost 30 inches.

the making of a quality fly line. I also learned a specific line can better your performance on the water. This has definitely been the case when I am pursuing trophy trout, when most of my presentations are quick and short. I use aggressive weight-forward tapers which are heavy enough to quickly load a fast-action rod. This and other match-ups taught me that fly lines are important weapons on the water.

In choosing the right fly line to hunt trophies, I make my selection based on the depth of the water I'm fishing. I also consider how long my casts need to be. The lines I prefer feature an aggressive head on the front part of the line. This aggressive diameter allows me to cast short, and load the rod quickly with excellent accuracy. It also allows me to get the maximum energy out of my rod if I need to cast a longer distance. This is especially effective in shallow water.

If I'm working deeper water with streamers, crayfish, or sculpin imitations, I turn to a sink-tip fly line with a moderate sinking rate, type 2 or 3. This allows me to get down in deeper holding waters, such as dark runs or pools. Such a line also helps me keep the pattern at a consistent depth when stripping them back. This allows my flies to look more natural. If conditions call

This night-time surprise is the most unusual kype I have ever seen on a brown. It doesn't even look real.

for scraping rocks in extremely deep water, a full-sinking line is effective in reaching holding fish.

"TAKE ME TO YOUR LEADER"

Fluorocarbon, fluorocarbon, *fluorocarbon!* Oh, did I mention fluorocarbon? From my perspective, fluorocarbon is the name of the game for leader and tippet material. I have been able to successfully fool and land more giant trout with fluorocarbon than with traditional extruded-nylon leader and tippet material. The advent of this material for fishing application during the 1990s was a huge bonus for me and all anglers who stalk smart and wary big fish in clear water.

Unlike regular nylon monofilament, fluorocarbon does not reflect light in the stream's surface and subsurface. Skittish fish are less likely to detect the angler's presence and presentation. Fluorocarbon is also extremely resistant to abrasion. This quality is invaluable when tussling with big fish around leader-grabbing snags. These two advantages have been the saving grace in many of my trophy trout encounters. Whether it is a huge brown dogging down trying to pull me around a rock or trying to fool a huge springtime bow into taking a size 20 midge, this material will allow you to rise to the challenge of catching the trout of your life.

An age-old "x" system is used to identify the diameter of monofilament or fluorocarbon. The larger the "x" designation, the smaller the diameter and lighter the material; the smaller the x, the heavier and larger the diameter. For example, 1x is normally 10-pound test and 5x is normally four-pound test. When hunting for trophy trout, I carry an assortment of 6x to 0x fluorocarbon leader and tippet material.

In rigging up for most western freestone rivers and tailwaters, I use 6x to 4x material. These waters are typically small, clear,

> ### AUTHOR'S TIP
>
> *When fighting large trout on a fly rod, you are applying only three to five pounds of pressure when your rod is flexed. Although it is difficult to imagine that huge trout can be caught with such terminal tackle, I have landed 10-pounders in short time on 6x tippet material.*

and full of big wary fish subjected to a parade of year-round pressure from anglers. The resident fish tend to be leader shy, so using fluorocarbon in this environment is an advantage. In contrast, many Midwestern rivers and waters in Alaska, a majority of the fish are migrating from large lakes or seas, where they have been subjected to little or no pressure from anglers, the relative lack of wariness permits the use of 4x to 2x tippets.

My advice is to carry leader and tippet material in a range of sizes and be sure it's new and it's fluorocarbon! With an assortment of sizes, you will be prepared for all types of fish and fishing conditions.

DON'T SPARE THE ROD

Sometimes I swear I was born with a Sage rod in my hand. I am sold on fast-action fly rods with well-thought-out tapers, and Sage delivers these designs consistently throughout their extensive product line.

I personally believe there is a huge advantage of being able to present a fly quickly to a trophy because such fish are so spooky—often you have only a few casts before the fish detects you. The more drifts you can get to a fish, the better chance you have that it will see and take your fly. A well-made, fast-action rod performs perfectly when quickness and accuracy matter. From time to time, some anglers ask me if an expensive rod is really worth the price. My response is always, "Yes." I have owned my 5-weight Sage XP for almost a decade and I have landed literally thousands of pounds of trout with it. I'll also tell you that it's the first fly rod I grab when performance counts. In my opinion, in the long run, it is worth the extra bucks. Time on the water has taught me that faster-action rods deliver superior results.

When dealing with large and powerful trophy trout, I prefer medium-fast and fast-action rods. The importance your rod will play in catching a giant is twofold: casting ability, and the speed and lifting strength when you are fighting a fish. Being able to apply enough pressure on a fish when you are fighting it shortens the length of the fight, increases your success rate, and help ensure the fish's safety. Also it gives you the chance to take control of the fight faster than you would with slow- or medium-action rods.

For 5- and 6-weight rods, I use a fast-action design that allow me the ability to apply enough pressure on the fish, allow me to load the rod fast, and be accurate at short distances.

For 7- and 8-weight rods, I use a medium-fast saltwater series. The reason I use such rods is that they are designed to be supple enough in the tip, allowing you to absorb powerful movements from the fish, as well as providing powerful lifting action in the lower section of the rod. This combination allows me to lift and turn big powerful fish. In most small tailwater or inlet drainages I use a 5- or 6-weight rod. These rods are strong enough to swiftly gain control in a fight, yet light enough to maintain accurate and, if needed, delicate presentations to the fish. I fish 7- or 8-weight medium-fast saltwater rods on larger bodies of water where distance and accuracy is the normal goal for casting, and for dealing with larger, powerful migratory fish in fast powerful currents.

Understanding what rod to use for each body of water and the fish that live in those waters will keep you one step ahead in landing that trophy. Casting to, hooking, lifting, and landing these giants is no easy task. Having a reliable rod eases the challenge.

THE REEL THING

Here's a question: Why buy a $400 reel if you're not going to let it do its job? I see so many anglers on the water fumbling by stripping in line with a large trout on the end. The result is often the fish is gone. Or they have the line wrapped around their head, reel, and the rod when the fish makes a bolting run and tink, the beast is off.

Fly-fishing reels are better now than they have ever been. Modern reels precision machined from a single block of bar-stock aluminum are designed to withstand constant pressure and strain from large, powerful fish. If you could ask a Mexican wahoo whipped by a Tibor or an Abel, it would probably agree. Although wahoo have been clocked swimming up to 50 miles an hour and can turn on a dime, they are defeated by the reel's ability to perform in these conditions because of unrelenting drag systems.

Even for subduing far less-berserk fish in fresh water, a fine reel is still a critical piece of gear in the complete setup suitable for catching trophy trout. A quality reel is determined by the slow start-up inertia necessary to withstand fast exploding runs and movement from the fish. Its components help in the performance of the reel. I prefer a cork–ball bearing disc drag or a ball bearing disc drag. These reels will allow for a smooth release of line, whether it's a short amount pulled form the reel during the powerful headshakes of the fish, or a long expanded run that could strip out numerous feet of line in a short period of time.

Make sure this drag system is sealed to allow the reel to perform well in the harshest weather conditions. Reels without a sealed drag system can freeze up in snowy or rainy conditions.

Last but not least, check the tension settings of the drag system to see if you can tighten down the tension enough to when you lift up your rod, you apply maximum pressure without the line releasing at the same time. You want the line to release only when the fish is applying pressure from its movements or actions. There are many good reels on the market. Choose the one you would trust to produce results when it counts. Make sure it has all of the above components and for sure performance on the water. For my money, it's a Ross reel.

NET GAIN

If it's big, you're in business. The more room and reach you have with a trout net, the better off you are. I own a net my friends have named the "Hog Pen." It's so big they had to ship it to me in a damn

In my experience, the most reliable fly reel on the planet along with my favorite dry fly.

crate. All right, I admit that is a bit much, but if you had seen the trout I have over the years, you too would want a net big enough to scoop up your fishing buddy as he floats by, beer-belly up. Besides, reaction to my jumbo net from fellow anglers adds humor to any trip.

"Expecting to hook Moby Dick?" goes one common line.

"Maybe flipper," I reply. "Hey, big fish insist on a big net. Gotta give 'em what they want."

A good net is probably the most overlooked tool for the job of catching a trophy trout. Having a net that can hold a fish of giant proportions can be the final determining factor in your success. I have three nets, each with a specific use. The smallest of the three has a basket measuring 20 inches long and 18 inches wide at the opening. And the other two are larger by a couple of inches. The largest of the three I use, the aforementioned Hog Pen, is an oversized net that has a basket measuring 21 inches wide and 27 inches long. The total length of the net is 62 inches.

The three characteristics of a net suited for pursuing trophy trout are 1) an opening large enough to handle fish with large bodies; 2) a mesh or rubberized deep basket, giving you the depth clearance to handle the length of the fish, and one that will not damage the fish's body when it is landed; and 3) a handle long enough for added reach, which increases your chances to successfully net your trophy.

WHEN OBESITY IS GOOD

All fish stories start with numbers or size. It's either how many fish you caught

My face and fingers weren't the only thing that was frozen stiff on this cold winter day.

I was sure jazzed to share this happy moment with Jay Harper when he landed his first 10-pound trout.

that day, or how big the fish was. A proper scale just puts some truth behind the story. I hear so many anglers say their fish weighed *this* much, and they didn't even have a scale. If you do land that 20-pound monster, wouldn't you want to scale to prove its actual size? Trust me, a good scale puts every thing into perspective!

Having a quality scale with you when catching trophy trout keeps you honest about your catch. It also takes the guessing out of the equation. Many anglers use the method of calculating the length and girth in a mathematical equation to determine the weight of their fish. While this method is accurate on normal proportioned fish, it does not compensate for the extreme proportions that these giants can grow.

I prefer a Chatelaine scale. This is a spring-loaded brass scale with of the capacity to weigh fish up to 30 pounds. It's easy to use and is equipped with a hook on one end, which I use to hook on the edge of the net, and a handle on the other end of the scale. Another feature is the adjustment knob at the top of the scale that allows you to zero out the scale when incorporating the weight of the net in the calculation (I hook my net to the scale and zero out the scale so that when I weigh the fish, the weight measurement will be an accurate representation of the fish's weight). This gives you to get the exact weight of the fish after you have landed it.

To properly use this scale when you land a trophy, simply hook this scale to the edge of the net and, with the fish in the net, lift the scale.

Another nice feature of the Chatelaine scale is its size: compact and light so it fits into the pocket of your fishing vest or the opening of a chest pack. By having this tool along the next time you go hunting for trophies, you will no longer wonder how big that giant really was. As mentioned, it also keeps you honest. It is very easy to look at a large fish and estimate the weight, only to find out you are several pounds off. I have had fish that I thought were heavier, based on the length and girth, but when I weighed them, the scale told a different story. I have also had fish that didn't appear to be as heavy as they were, but again, the scale provides an accurate assessment.

THE SUNSHINE RULE

The importance of having a long-billed hat is to reduce the amount of glare off the surface of the water and the light from above. The two things you want your hat to have to reduce light glare are first, a long or broad-brim that casts a shadow over your face and eliminates glare, as well as keeping the light from hitting your eyes. The second thing is to look for in a functional hat is a black or dark coloration on the underside of the bill. This won't reflect light and also helps reduce the amount of glare, enabling you better vision into the water.

SMILE FOR THE CAMERA

With the advancement of pictures and photography going from film to digital, the advantages of capturing that special moment when you have landed a trophy is one that can be treasured forever with the use of a good camera. The possibilities are endless. Now, with the additional help of Adobe Photoshop or Photoshop elements, you can easily enhance an image even if the exposure or composition is slightly off.

It's true what they say that a picture is worth a thousand words. I love reliving each fish and the experience I had catching it by reviewing my own pictures, and my guess is so will you.

Today there are many, many affordable quality cameras on the market to choose from. For the last four years, I have used a waterproof Pentax Optio digital camera. The waterproof feature makes this camera an excellent choice around water. Plus the camera has high pixel rating up to seven megapixels, which allows quality pictures in large sizes, not to mention the cool underwater shots it can take!

I have used larger 35mm cameras as well, from a Nikon D5, to a Cannon Rebel XT. And I must say the new Cannon cameras have some great color saturation. However, these are still big cameras. If you drop them in the drink you are in trouble. If I am taking photos exclusively and not fishing, then I prefer to have a 35mm around my neck. But if I am fishing, I always carry my compact, waterproof camera. Remember, the higher the megapixels, the better the resolution.

Don't forget the camera on your next trip for trophy trout. For one who is addicted to traveling light, a camera is the one non-essential piece of gear that is definitely worth hauling along. Weeks, months, and tears later, taking time to capture the moment will help you relive one of your most exhilarating fishing experiences again and again.

I was afraid this dog was going to take a bite out of the camera. No wonder big flies scare up big browns.

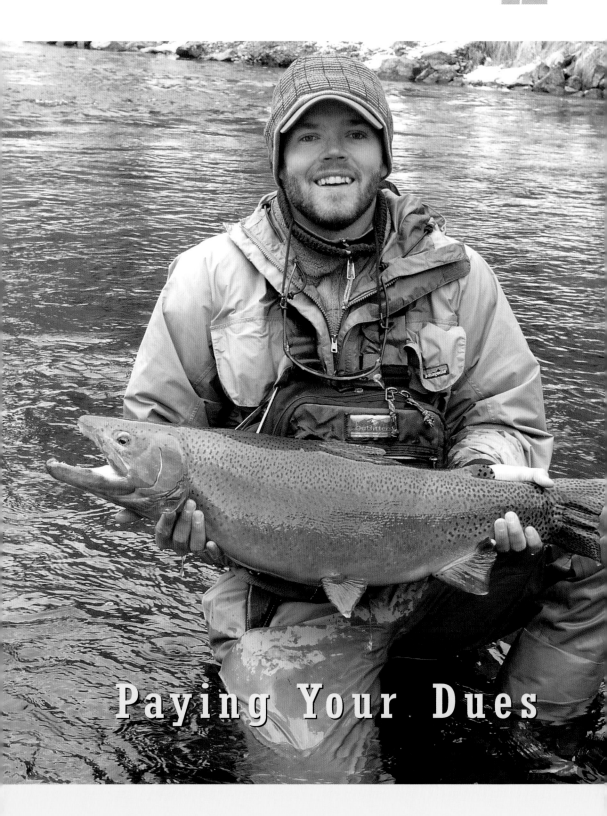

Paying Your Dues

TO SUCCESSFULLY CATCH TROPHY TROUT, you first have to time it right—be there in your waders when the giants are in the river and active.

While I have enjoyed many successful days, as evidenced by the photographs in this book, there are also many days when I have searched for big trout without so much as a spooked fish. Through countless cups of coffee, driving all night, and storms that were so bad that I wondered if it was even possible to cast in these conditions, praying I was going to make it back alive and in one piece.

While many anglers get frustrated and discouraged on trips that don't produce, I prefer to look at these days as paying my dues.

My sincere advice is this: Have faith that by working hard and learning new things on each trip, you will be rewarded in the future. Nothing in fishing is predictable. Maybe you'll be rewarded sooner than you imagine. On slow days I make a point to run through all the little circumstances of the day, determining if something is different from years past. This has been a learning tool to better understand trout behavior, migrating patterns, and areas where they may be holding. If I didn't take the time to pay my dues and continue to learn, I wouldn't fully understand when or where to catch the fish.

In this chapter I'll share some stories of trips in the past that ended in success—and some that didn't. But on each of these days, regardless of the outcome, I was rewarded with fresh understanding, even if it didn't seem obvious at the time. I hope that you too, will gain some insight and knowledge from my adventures and misadventures.

FALL'S HIDDEN TREASURE

When I discuss reading water, I am always reminded of October 12, 2004. It was a bright sunny day with a clear sky— quite honestly, less-than-ideal conditions

and conditions I certainly would not order up when pursuing brown trout. Cloudy, storm-filled conditions are normally better this time of year when trying to catch giant browns. Unsettled weather gives these bruisers cover and encourages them to move about the water much more than on bright sunny days.

The night before I called my brother, Sean, who had just returned to the United States after living in Japan. I hadn't fished with him in a year. I was excited to tell him about the conditions and to get back on the water with my longtime fishing partner

"How's fishing, bro?" he asked.

"It's been unreal, we have some of the highest water we've seen in years, and the browns are thick in the river, I said. "I'm getting all jazzed up just thinking about it. You need to get your skinny butt to the river with me in the next few days."

After telling him a few more stories of some of the great fish caught in past few days, I convinced him to meet me at the river early the next afternoon following my half-day morning guide trip.

While assisting my happy clients find and land several decent-sized fish between 20 and 22 inches, I also noticed telltale signs of a few larger fish moving around. Around 1 o'clock I hooked up with my brother and we headed to a stretch of shallow, riffled water where I had seen numerous large fish moving earlier in the week. Sure enough, when we arrived, there was a big brightly colored brown feeding actively in an even-moving riffle.

It had been a while since we fished together in the fall. I had a smirk on my face because I knew he was going to freak out when saw the size of these bad-ass browns. It looked like a good fish for my brother to try. It only took three drifts. The fish opened its jaw and my brother set the hook to the white glint of its mouth.

"Fish on!" we both hollered in unison.

The big brown erupted, thrashing wildly on the surface, and racing downstream toward some large boulders studding the river. Just then Sean looked over at me in a daze. He couldn't believe the size of this heavily spotted brown, partly due to the fact when trophy trout explode out of the water they always look even bigger than their actual size.

Early season trout show their true colors: a fine postcard-quality specimen of *Salmo trutta*.

If I didn't land another brown for the rest of my life after catching this monster, I would die a happy man.

"What are you waiting for?" I yelled. "Run after him! He quickly gained his composure and got down to business. I coached my brother as he franticly worked the fish around and past the obstacles. One large rock had an undercut. The fish went under the rock and tried to wrap the leader around it to break free. Just then I saw an enormous shadow bolt upstream from beneath the rock. I was startled—it was a different fish. It was so large it nearly took my breath away.

That was a monster, I thought to myself. But I stayed focused and continued to help my brother fight his trophy. A few minutes later Sean was holding a striking 24-inch male brown. It was the highlight of his day.

Sean then looked up at me and said: "Man, you weren't kidding. These browns are unreal!"

That was a proud moment for me. It's not every day your big brother looks up at you in awe about something you discovered. High five and a few pictures later, we released my brother's beautiful fish. He was all smiles.

"You're up," he said. Music to my ears after seeing that monster shadow dart out from the undercut. We returned to the area where I saw the huge shadow. Was the fish still in the area? I began the search. It wasn't long before I found him holding at a drop-off point where a shallow riffle turned into a deep run.

With a huge pointed jaw and enormous orange fins extending out from its body, the trout looked like a giant golden alligator. I took a deep breath. It took me a while to reach the water depth where the brown was holding. After applying a few more split-shots to my rig, I was confident I was feeding him perfectly. A few casts later the fish turned sideways, opened its big kype, and my fly disappeared.

I waited a split second for his jaws to close and then I reared back. Immediately it started doing the most aggressive head-shakes I had ever felt on a 5-weight fly rod. Once it broke the surface I got a real good look.

"Oh my God," were the first words out of my mouth. It was massive. "I have the big one on!" I yelled to my brother.

He came running over to watch the show. "No pressure" he replied jokingly, but it didn't faze me a bit. I knew I was in the zone. The fish took a few long runs, but kept his head down and dogged me continuously. Numerous times I corked my rod to turn the fish, triggering fierce headshakes. Then the fish pointed his head back down and continued fighting me.

Ten minutes later and a couple hundred yards downstream, I finally slid the giant brown trout into my net. The fish measured 30 inches long and weighed 11 pounds—the current International Game Fish Association's Colorado state record for brown trout on four-pound test.

Ever since that day I've been impressed at how such a large trout was hiding in such a small area underneath that rock. Needless to say, I now literally leave no rock unturned when pursuing giant browns. This story and many others are great examples of how elusive large trout can be hiding in areas where they can feed free from stress. Reading water and trying to understand where fish are holding is a huge advantage when trying to find your trophy.

AFTERNOON DELIGHT

The morning had been cold and cloudless. By noon I'd fished a section of the Taylor River several times with just one mid-sized rainbow to show for it. The bright sunlight had made the fish wary and all of the large fish I'd seen in recent days seemed to have vanished. But I had this weird gut feeling that something memorable was going to play out today.

Dark cloud cover rolled in after lunch, dulling the reflection on the water. This gave me excellent visibility for sighting fish. I finally spotted two big 'bows holding midstream in front of a large boulder. When I moved in closer to plop the fly in front of what looked like a 10-pounder, I spotted movement just upstream. As I focused on the spot, I could make out the telltale red side and gill plate of a monstrous rainbow— I estimated its weight to be in the mid teens. It was so big it looked like it didn't belong in the skinny water it was holding in.

Quickly, I ducked down, so my silhouette against the snowy background would not spook the huge fish. Just as I prepared to cast, the fish suddenly slid several feet upstream, and in a flash his spot was taken over by an even larger male!

I stood there, locked in position, afraid that any movement would frighten either one of the pair of monster trout now holding just upstream from me. Gently, I tossed a roll cast to the closest fish. I was slightly short, so I stripped out another two feet of line and cast again.

On my third cast, the current took the midge pattern right into the trout's feeding lane. The big fish kicked a little to the side, opened his mouth wide, and took the fly. I set the hook and the surface erupted in crazed headshakes. Water flew four to five feet in all directions. With each terrific shake, my rod- arm pumped wildly up and down like I was hammering nails.

The giant rainbow bolted upstream with me following as closely as I could. I caught up with him but he turned and charged downstream. This up-and-down battle lasted for 10 minutes or so, until he finally tired and made several sideways rolls on the surface. Only then was I able to guide him into shallow water. Still, after this frenzied fight the bruiser continued to thrust away every time I went to net him head first. Finally positioned downstream of the leviathan, with the help of the rivers current, I slid him headfirst into my outstretched net. The incredible fish measured 32 inches and 16 pounds—one of the largest rainbow trout I'd ever landed.

I was pumped after landing this big boy, but the two fish swimming with him were bigger than he was!

I did it: I captured two beauties in one shot. What a day.

Talk about tired! I was exhausted from franticly chasing this rampaging beast upstream and down. Without a doubt, though, it was a good price to pay for such an awesome 'bow.

On some days when you least expect it, a touch of magic happens. Fish hard all day, even if you are not seeing much. You never know—they could be lurking around the next bend.

HIT 'EM WHERE THEY AIN'T

Anyway you view it, the excitement and thrill of casting to a trophy trout and watching it to take your fly is an exhilarating rush. This visual aspect of nymphing truly is an art. I am always reminded of this story when I think of spotting fish.

I was on a trip in upstate New York in pursuit of trophy browns. It was late October and the third day of my week-long trip. The fish were thick in the water. I had luckily stumbled into one of the largest runs of giant browns in recent years. On this day the water was off color from rain the night before. To make matters worse, the day was partly cloudy, and the reflection of the white clouds on the surface of the water made it even harder to spot fish.

I spent the first few hours of the day casting into readable water and picking up a few fish. I could blind cast only so long, before I was bored out of my mind, so I decided to walk upstream. I was scanning the water when I came across a bend where a shallow riffle flowed into a drop-off run about four feet deep. I noticed numerous white-looking objects. At first glance they looked like pieces of light river bottom, stones, or gravel perhaps.

Do you ever have those moments when you are on the water and are not quite sure what you're seeing is a trout, but since you are not convinced either way, you don't want to leave? This was one of those times.

When I sharpened my focus and stared at the same spot for several minutes, I saw one of the white objects extend and become larger in size. I was looking at the ivory insides of fish jaws. The run was full of large male brown trout—what a find.

I ended up getting a 10-pound, a 12-pound, and a 14-pound brown trout from that area. The secret was focusing on the jaws of the huge trout to know when to set the hook. This experience taught me that you don't always see the whole trout. The ability to pinpoint where the fish are, even if you don't have a full view, can turn a slow day into an action-packed one.

HEAD-ON COLLISION

The scene was set: a perfect scenario for catching a large rainbow trout. The fish was holding in a shallow shelf downstream of a large, deep-running pool. The trout was moving up and down and side to side in a feeding free-for-all. The conditions seemed almost too perfect. *This fish's days are numbered,* I thought to myself.

"Which side?" I asked my fishing companion, Matt.

"The left side of the run," he replied. Because there was significant glare on the water, I needed to know which side of the river would be the best approach and knowing Matt had a clear view of the fish, I relied on his judgment.

There are so many advantages to fishing with a skilled partner. You can both collectively put your heads together and figure out the best way to cast to and catch these large trout.

"Go for it man." he said. "Let's stick this pig."

I crept into position to make a cast, and to my surprise, the fish ate on my first drift. *This is meant to be,* I thought. *It's not every day the fish eats on the first drift.*

Once the fish took the fly, it started

shaking and then bolted upstream to the deeper run. The flow was strong. This upped the tactical ante—landing this fish in this deep fast-moving water would be a challenge. Little did I know this wasn't the extent of my problems. There was more trouble to come.

Among my regular fishing partners, the guy not fighting the fish acts like a copilot and coaches the guy with the fish throughout the fight. About half way through the battle Matt said to me in a confused voice, "Uh, Landon, watch out, dude."

"Watch out for what?" I asked. To this day his response makes me laugh.

"Dude, I hate to break the news, but there's a tree coming at you."

My eyes were riveted on the fish. I tore my eyes away for a split second and glanced over my shoulder at Matt.

He was desperately pointing to the top of the run where, no lie, bobbing downstream was a log that looked like the base of a tree about 15 feet long.

How in the world am I going to get out of this mess? I wondered. In warp speed I tried

Eric lifts another monster for the camera—one of three fish of its size we nailed in late spring.

to figure a creative way out, and brilliantly came up with nothing. There was no escape. My eyes flashed back and forth between the fish and the approaching tree; every ominous foot the log came closer, it felt like minutes passing.

You know the ending, of course. Tree hits Landon, Landon goes swimming, and the fish makes a clean getaway. The end result of the tree in the water has two perspectives: For me, I was the victim. For the fish, it was a blessing. No matter which way you look at it, it's a comical story, one that is still trotted out for a laugh among my friends and family.

FEELING BY LANTERN LIGHT

Fly fishing at night is a unique experience. Normal sight vanishes; sound and feel become the primary senses. You must rely on what you know about a piece of water during daylight hours. You never fully know what's lurking out there in the dark.

One of my first night-time adventures was with Eric Mondragen, a long-time friend. We had discussed going after big fish at night. We knew that trout, especially browns, when hard-pressed have been known to shift their foraging to a nocturnal setting, ambushing prey and actively feeding under the cover of night. In the popular Colorado tailwaters fished heavily during the day, this phenomenon might just be happening. It would give the resident giants a chance to move about without dodging the crowds in waders.

We decided to head up to the legendary Frying Pan River to hunt trophies by moonlight. We packed up our gear, including lanterns, head lamps, and a pint of peach schnapps to bring us warmth in the bone-chilling dark. We set out in the early evening hours to get to the water by 9 p.m. With coffee flowing and the energy level remaining high we finally arrived at the river.

We decided to start fishing directly below Rudi reservoir in a famous hole called the toilet bowl. This is a deep swirling pool that in high water takes on the look of a giant flushing bowl. It's an unusual section of water to say the least. Located at the bottom release of the reservoir, the water at times is full of mysis shrimp, along with open-mouthed trout known to exceed 20 pounds.

I had heard stories of anglers doing well here at night. With the thought of a 20-pounder straining my rod to its butt, I was ready to fish till dawn. We suited up, turned on our head lamps and lantern, took a good-luck swig, and Eric said, "Let's do this, man."

Eureka—there they were two large rainbows right on the edge of the run feeding like mad. I told Eric he was up; it didn't take him long to get his fly wet.

I had waded only a few steps up to the top of the run and starting casting when Eric screamed out, "I got him!"

This might be the start of something awesome, I thought.

Eric was freaking out, acting like a little kid ripping into the pile of presents under the tree. I was pumped and glad he hooked this toad—for sure the largest trout he had ever seen. It was eerie. Each time the monster ran to the other side of the bowl, everything would disappear into the night. Eric was relying 100 percent on feel.

The fight was quick. Five minutes later the big 'bow was ready for mesh—a beautiful female tipping nine pounds on the scale. Eric was ecstatic. After a few pictures he slid the big fish back to the run to join other trophies roaming the mysterious, dark pool. I looked up and said, "I know this pic is going to make a great story someday."

AFTERWORD

In my years of pursuing giant trout, I have gained a wealth of knowledge about fly fishing and quite the storybook along the way. The excitement of this aquatic hunt, and having friends to share it with, is without a doubt what keeps me coming back for more. Fishing wouldn't be as much fun without a story to tell and a friendship built along the way.

I know you will find knowledge, excitement, and determination in this book. It's been an unbelievable ride for me and others over the years. I wish the same for you in pursuit of magnificent trophy trout. Good fishing!

INDEX

Photography Credits

Burger, John page: 141

Drummond, Angus pages: 13, 20, 76, 83, 91, 104,

Extreme Fly Fishing (Dennis Kreutz) pages: 14, 31, 36, 80, 94, 112, 133–134, 138, 142

Miller, Scottie pages: 11

Martin, Frank pages: main cover photo, 6, 93

Mayer, Landon pages: 8, 17, 22, 25, 27–28, 32, 34, 40–41, 43–44, 46, 49–50, 55–56, 63, 66, 68, 72, 75, 79, 86, 92, 98, 103, 107–108, 110–111, 117–118, 120–121, 137, 144, 147– 148, 150,

Mayer, Sean page: 145

YOU'VE READ THE BOOK
NOW WATCH THE ACTION

Landing the Trout of Your Life
A spectacular new how-to fishing video brings all the action to life
With Landon Mayer
Featuring John Barr

"Landing trophy trout doesn't have to be a once in a lifetime chance," says Landon Mayer, author of **How to Catch the Biggest Trout of Your Life**. "With the right skill and training, it can become a lifetime of chances!"

In *Landing the Trout of Your Life*, Landon teams with John Barr, legendary fly creator, to bring this gospel to life. Using tried and true principles and techniques, Landon and John demonstrate how you can spot, hook, and land trophy trout in your favorite river.

This full-length, ground-breaking teaching DVD includes some of the most captivating fly-fishing footage ever captured. From 10-pound rainbows caught in the heart of Colorado, to 16-pound monster browns from the rivers of upstate New York, Landon and John pull out all the stops in order to bring you some of the most exciting fish fights the sport has ever seen. You'll experience first hand why Landon has become one of the most sought-after fishing guides in the country.

So come along for the adventure. And hang on for the ride of your life!

To order copies of the DVD *Landing the Trout of Your Life*, send a check (or telephone with credit card information) in the amount of $29.95 each plus $5 shipping and handling ($15 to addresses outside the U.S.) to:

Wild River Press
Post Office Box 13360
Mill Creek, Washington 98082
USA
Telephone 425-486-3638
www.wildriverpress.com

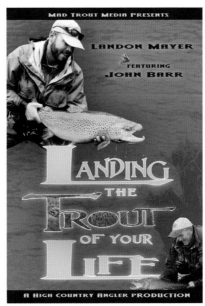